ASPECTS OF LAW AFFECTING THE PARAMEDICAL PROFESSIONS

ASPECTS OF LAW AFFECTING THE PARAMEDICAL PROFESSIONS

John D. Finch BA, BCL
Senior Lecturer in Law, Faculty of Law, Leicester University

ff
faber and faber
LONDON · BOSTON

First published in 1984
by Faber and Faber Limited
3 Queen Square, London WC1N 3AU
Set by Goodfellow & Egan Typesetting Ltd
Printed in Great Britain by
Redwood Burn Ltd, Trowbridge

British Library Cataloguing in Publication Data

Finch, John D.
Aspects of law affecting the paramedical professions.
1. Law—Great Britain 2. Allied health personnel—Legal status, laws, etc.—
Great Britain
I. Title
344.1′0024616 KD665.A4

ISBN 0-571-13272-3

CONTENTS

PREFACE

This book aims at a balance between the interests and requirements of paramedical practitioners engaged in practice within the National Health Service and all those who are not so engaged but who are practising in the independent health care sector, in other employment, or on their own account.

The topics selected for discussion are those which are considered to be of most immediate and frequent concern to paramedical practitioners in general. In the discussion of many legal questions in this book the reader will encounter common ground with medical practice, which the activities of paramedical professions supplement in so many ways. Where necessary, however, the separate legal incidents of paramedical practice will be specifically indicated within this common ground.

Legal sources such as statutes, regulations and the decisions of the courts are directly cited, but the text is designed to be useful to practitioners who have no particular familiarity with a legal system. Footnotes are kept to a minimum throughout. The text remains, however, a text about legal regulation of professional activity and the sources of the relevant rules are indicated whenever necessary. A brief explanation of sources of law is given in the introductory chapter.

The contents of this book represent the law applicable in England and Wales, though the greater part of it applies throughout the United Kingdom as a whole. Scots law and the law in force in Northern Ireland differ in certain respects from the law of England

and Wales, but it is not within the scope of this book to account for such differences.

In other European countries as well as elsewhere in the world, legal rules and principles may differ greatly from those examined in this book. Readers are therefore reminded to make a careful check on the laws affecting their professional lives to which they may be subject in such other countries.

ACKNOWLEDGEMENTS

The author of a book is always fortunate to receive comments and suggestions from those who are experts in their own fields. In this regard I owe a particular debt of gratitude to the following people: to Dr Brian Donald, Registrar of the Council for Professions Supplementary to Medicine, for his detailed perusal of Chapter 2 (registration and associated issues) and Chapter 3 (discipline); to Mr Stephen Woolfe of Leicester, solicitor, for his valuable comments on Chapter 4 (employment law); and to Miss Marquita Inman, Lecturer in Law at Leicester University for her very helpful scrutiny of Chapter 10 (evidence).

I wish also to express my thanks to Miss P. A. Downie FCSP, who as Medical and Nursing Editor of Faber and Faber has made a number of useful suggestions on the presentation of the text of this book, and who prepared the select bibliography and list of useful addresses.

John Finch, 1984

ABBREVIATIONS AND GLOSSARY

REFERENCES TO LAW REPORTS

The following abbreviations will be found with reference to cases decided by the courts and which create precedents. The reports and journals whose full titles are now given may be found in most good libraries, and should certainly be found in libraries attached to establishments of higher education in which law is taught.

AC	Appeal Cases
All ER	All England Reports
ICR	Industrial Court Reports
ITR	Industrial Tribunal Reports
KB	King's Bench Division
LGR	Local Government Reports
NZLR	New Zealand Law Reports
QB	Queen's Bench Division
SJ	Solicitors' Journal
SLT	Scots Law Times
TLR	Times Law Reports
WLR	Weekly Law Reports

(Any other occasional case reference abbreviations found in the text relate to cases reported so very long ago, and in such relatively obscure reports, that readers of this book would be highly unlikely to require recourse to the original report.)

GLOSSARY OF LEGAL AND OTHER TERMS

The following notes on legal and other terms found in the text are not intended to replace the descriptions of those terms when they are encountered in their relevant context. They are intended as a provisional guide only.

assault The reasonable apprehension by a person of the immediate infliction of unlawful bodily contact; a term frequently used to refer to the actual contact, which is strictly speaking in terms of the non-criminal law a *battery* (see below); certain physical assaults are also criminal offences.

battery The intentional and direct application of force (which for legal purposes includes any unpermitted physical contact) to another person.

case-law The rules and principles resulting from the judicial determination of disputes which have reached the stage of a court hearing, and which create precedents depending on a variety of factors including the level of the court which makes the decision.

closure In the particular context in which this term is used in this book, the policy of restricting professional practice to those appropriately qualified or registered.

common law Historically, the law which became common to the whole of England; but in the context of this book, law which results from judicial decisions as distinct from legislation or regulations.

infamous conduct A term now normally replaced in common parlance by the term 'serious professional misconduct' and meaning such conduct as will not be tolerated by disciplinary bodies within the relevant professional registering body or organisation.

plaintiff The person who commences legal proceedings against another; in the context of this book with the normal object of obtaining damages, though in some instances with the aim of being awarded an injunction to restrain the future behaviour of the person complained about.

scope The area or delineation of professional practice which may have implications for both professional discipline and for legal standards of care.

statute An Act of Parliament.

statutory instrument (S.I.) A regulation made, for instance by a Government department, to regulate a particular area of activity, within powers conferred for that purpose by appropriate legislation.

subpoena A legal writ commanding a person to appear and give evidence, and possibly also to bring with him certain documents.

tort A civil (that is, non-criminal) wrong which may be committed independently of any breach of contract or breach of trust, and the results of which may be compensated by the award of damages, or by the issuing of an injunction, or both.

trespass The tort of which, in addition to trespass to land, assault, battery and certain forms of unlawful detention are examples.

writ An official (royal) legal document which instructs that something shall or shall not be done.

Chapter One

SOURCES OF LAW

The law affecting paramedical practice and practitioners is a hybrid between rules and regulations which are applicable to paramedical practitioners alone, and rules and regulations which are of general application but which include paramedical practice within their general purview. Aside from the law itself, though frequently influencing it and interacting with it, are ethical principles. An example of such a principle is the professional obligation to maintain the confidentiality of the relationship between practitioner and patient or client. Such non-legal considerations are themselves of general application but may none the less be given a particular shape or significance in the paramedical context in which they are raised.

Since a substantial number of those readers who use this book will be registered practitioners, the structure of the system of state registration and its professional and disciplinary implications are considered in some detail in the two following chapters. As will be seen however from the subject-matter of the remaining chapters, the concern of this book is by no means limited to state registered paramedical practice. Those two chapters apart, therefore, the concern of this book is with all paramedical practice whether state registered or not.

In the remaining chapters, which examine health and safety, employment law, duties of care, the safety of premises, consent, confidentiality, evidence and records, it will from time to time be necessary to consider the implications of state registration for the general law. For example, the law of employment which is examined in Chapter 4 contains necessary reference to restrictive legal provisions governing the employment of paramedical practitioners in the National Health Service (p. 55). And in the case of unjustified disclosure of information in breach of confidence or inconsistently with the practitioner-patient relationship, certain restrictions are specifically provided for by the statements of 'infamous conduct in a professional respect' issued by the registration boards for the professions supplementary to medicine (p. 46).

Whether the subject-matter of this book relates at any given point solely to state registered practice, or whether it relates more widely to paramedical practice in general, the sources of legal regulation are common. These sources are now briefly examined.

STATUTES

The most authoritative form of legal regulation in our legal system is an Act of Parliament, or statute. It is said that Parliament can make or unmake any law whatsoever. There may sometimes be constitutional limitations, for instance those resulting from European Community law, which influence what Parliament is recognised as enacting as valid law. But provided Parliament acts validly according to the rules and principles which control the process of legislation itself, what it enacts is the supreme source of law in our legal system. Any judicial decision, or decision of a court of law, can be overturned by legislation. And any subordinate legislation in the form, for instance, of regulations will be of no effect if inconsistent with the provisions of a statute. Judicial decisions and subordinate legislation are briefly discussed in a moment.

Central to the system of state registered paramedical practice is the Professions Supplementary to Medicine Act 1960. The provisions of this statute and of rules made pursuant to it are discussed in detail in Chapters 2 and 3. A statute which is of common application in any field or type of paramedical practice is the Occupiers' Liability Act of 1957, discussed in Chapter 8. Examples of statutes which are of such general application could of course be multiplied. These two statutes are noted here, however, in order to give examples of the highest source of legal regulation both in matters concerning a specific field of activity and matters of general concern which are not so confined. In both instances the statute constitutes the bare bones on to which the flesh is put from other sources. Those other sources principally include orders and regulations made under powers given by the 'parent' statute, and judicial decisions which give a meaning to statutory provisions in a case which arises as the result of a particular dispute.

In the two examples which have just been chosen as illustrations, how is the 'flesh' put on to the bare bones provided by the particular statute in question? The Professions Supplementary to Medicine Act of 1960 is amplified principally by Orders in Council regulating such matters as registration, discipline and appeals from disciplinary committees. Judicial decisions play their part also, in particular on the question of the practical meaning of 'serious professional misconduct' (otherwise known as 'infamous conduct'). In the case of the Occupiers' Liability Act 1957, elaboration of the basic rules of the statute is effected in particular cases by judicial decisions. Examples of such decisions determining disputes in particular cases will be used to illustrate the law relating to the safety of premises which is examined in Chapter 8.

One particular point to note in relation to statute law is that the Crown – generally speaking government and state agencies and organisations – is subject to special rules. Statutes do not bind the Crown unless they are specifically expressed to do so, or unless they do so by necessary implication from the nature of their provisions.

The Occupiers' Liability Act does bind the Crown. But there are some statutes to be examined in this book which do not extend to the Crown, and which therefore require special mention for a particular reason. That is, that the National Health Service is a Crown activity, and so a statute which does not bind the Crown does not extend to National Health Service activities.

Instances to be examined in later chapters are employment legislation (Chapter 4), not all of which applies to the NHS; and health and safety enforcement powers (Chapter 6).

Subordinate legislation

Regulations and orders may be made under powers provided in the principal or 'parent' statute in order to amplify and elaborate on the central basic structure set out in the Act. The term 'statutory instrument' (S.I.) is a comprehensive expression applicable to subordinate legislation in all its forms. There are two categories of statutory instrument, both of which are encountered in this book. One category is that of legislative powers conferred on the Queen in Council and which are stated in the parent Act to be 'exercisable by Order in Council'. The other category is that of legislative powers which are conferred on a Minister and which are stated in the parent Act to be exercisable by way of statutory instrument.

As noted above, the Professions Supplementary to Medicine Act of 1960 is amplified and given further practical effect by Orders in Council. Where powers concern only one particular department of Government it is normal for the parent Act to provide that powers to make subordinate legislation in the form of regulations shall be exercisable by a named Minister. Such, for instance, is the case of regulations restricting paramedical employment in the National Health Service to state registered practitioners.

Subordinate legislation, though in its very nature more detailed than the parent statute providing for its creation, may itself require further 'interpretation' by the courts in order to make it apply to a particular problem case. It is to judicial decisions as a source of law that attention now turns.

Judicial decisions

When a dispute arises as to the application of a particular rule or rules to an individual case it is frequently necessary to take legal proceedings resulting in the determination of the issue by a court. Judicial decisions, or the decisions of judges in such cases, serve both to determine the particular dispute between the parties and to set precedents which may, and in some cases must, be followed in future cases in the absence of some good and legally recognised reason for not doing so.

Strictly speaking, precedents are only set by the decisions of the higher courts, that is the Court of Appeal and the House of Lords. An appeal to the House of Lords is a relatively rare event, and fewer than 100 such appeals take place in any one year. Appeals to the Court of Appeal are much more frequent, numbering about 2500 annually. Owing to a combination of their relative frequency in comparison with House of Lords' decisions and their binding effect by way of precedent on all the lower courts, a substantial proportion of the cases cited in this book will be found to emanate from the Court of Appeal.

Decisions of the High Court, that is the level of the judicial hierarchy below the Court of Appeal, do not create binding precedents but are considered as exercising a persuasive and influential effect on later judicial decisions at the same level of authority. Needless to say, the decision of a High Court judge cannot bind the Court of Appeal by way of precedent. Nor can a decision of the Court of Appeal have any binding effect on future decisions of the House of Lords. The House of Lords will normally regard itself as bound by its own previous decisions, unless there are very pressing reasons – for instance of considerable social change over the years – to depart from an earlier decision.

Lest it be wondered why there is not a rule to fit every case which arises in practice, the nature of judicial activity should be considered. In the case of both statutes and statutory instruments the foresight of Parliament and of the subordinate legislator is necessarily limited, and it is clear that by no means all cases can be legislated for in advance. In the case of judicial decisions, the position is in a sense reversed. It is unnecessary for a court of law to exercise foresight in providing for specific future cases, though of course judges are mindful of the consequences which their decisions are likely to have in practice. A judicial determination of a disputed case is always retrospective in so far as the conditions upon which the judicial process is to operate have already been created. They consist of the circumstances of the disputed issue, and it is that dispute which the court is principally concerned to resolve.

Judges, and especially those in the Court of Appeal and the House of Lords, will often make statements which are not strictly necessary to arrive at a decision in the particular case in hand but which are nevertheless of great value in giving future direction to the area of law in which the dispute has arisen. Such statements may consist either of generalisations concerning the rules in question or of additional observations going deliberately beyond the bounds of the instant dispute. Such wider statements made by appeal courts will not necessarily bind lower courts to arrive at particular results in future cases which they are called upon to determine. But they will exercise a very persuasive influence on the outcome of a case if they are considered by the judge in that later case to be relevant to the facts in issue.

Although a particular dispute needs to become the subject of judicial proceedings if the judges are to have an opportunity to determine the issue and maybe lay down a rule of law in so doing, judicial decision-making and judicial precedent is by no means a piecemeal process. On the contrary, reports of judicially decided cases exist to enable judges to be presented with rules and principles established in other cases. A table of cases cited in this book is on pages 199–201; and a key to the abbreviations used in citing such cases will be found on page 13. By constant reference to previous judicial decisions the courts come to build up bodies of precedent. It thus becomes possible to say, for instance, that 'the law is going in a certain direction', or that such and such 'represents the present state of the law'.

HEALTH CIRCULARS AND NOTICES

Health circulars (HC) and health notices (HN) are issued to health authorities within the National Health Service for a great variety of administrative and guidance purposes. In many cases a circular or notice will explain recent legislation or case law as it is envisaged to apply to NHS activities and operations. Circulars and notices, though of vital operational importance, are certainly not sources of law in the sense that legislation, subordinate legislation and judicial decisions are sources of law. They nevertheless represent the immediate guidance upon which officers and employees of the NHS frequently base or alter their actions. They are important guides to what may, and in many cases must, be done in order to comply with the law.

There is one specific type of situation in which the contents of a circular or notice may indirectly represent the source of a legal obligation. That is the case, noted in Chapter 5 (p. 86), in which staff are alerted to a particular hazard or danger. If, having received reasonable notice of the danger in question, staff take no action to avoid its occurrence or recurrence in future, such failure could lead to an action for negligence if someone was injured as a result.

CODES OF PRACTICE

Of a somewhat different order still as a source of guidance are codes of practice. Such codes may be encountered in connection with a great variety of pursuits and occupations. Codes of practice are encountered in Chapter 6 in the context of health and safety at work.

Codes of practice do not themselves impose legal obligations as such, but they are an important source of practical guidance as to what is, and what is not, acceptable practice in the particular areas of activity to which they relate. As will be explained at the appropriate place, a departure from accepted and acceptable practice as set out in a code of practice may be evidence of falling below a required standard of care and therefore of negligence. The effect of ignoring the requirements of a code of practice may therefore be compared with that of ignoring a hazard warning, noted above.

Some codes of practice may receive the approval of the Health and Safety Commission pursuant to powers given by the Health and Safety at Work Act 1974. Though a code of this special type does not of itself impose legal rights and duties, it will be explained in Chapter 6 that a breach of the provisions of an approved code of practice is taken in most cases as evidence of breach of a duty imposed by regulations to which the code relates. The provisions of such a code therefore come very close to constituting a source of law in their own right.

Chapter Two

THE PROFESSIONS SUPPLEMENTARY TO MEDICINE

REGISTRATION AND THE STATUTORY FRAMEWORK

The principal sources of law affecting professional practice and conduct to be discussed in this book have been outlined in general terms. It is now time to move directly to the specific laws, orders and regulations which govern the statutory structure of the professions supplementary to medicine. The governing statute is the Professions Supplementary to Medicine Act 1960.

Professionalisation and the variety of professions

The wide variety of professional, specialist and skilled activities which supplement medical practice is such that a single scheme of organisation is not easy to create. Indeed, many professional activities supplementary to medicine remain outside the legal structure to be examined in this chapter.

A recent article [1] specifically on the subject of the professions which are, in statutory terms under the 1960 Act, supplementary to medicine also lists the remaining descriptions of professional and technical staff working in the National Health Service in a variety of 'paramedical' occupations. In addition to those whose professional and disciplinary structure is the subject of this chapter, such other 'paramedical' occupations which are listed include: chaplains, pharmacists, dental assistants and technicians, scientists including biochemists, physicists and psychologists, various physiological technicians, opticians, dark room technicians and speech therapists, as well as a variety of other helpers and technical staff.

The DHSS statistics referred to in this article in fact include medical laboratory scientific officers under the heading 'Technicians', and include chiropodists, dietitians, occupational therapists, orthoptists, physiotherapists and remedial gymnasts naturally under the title 'Professions Supplementary to Medicine'. In the scheme legislated by the Professions Supplementary to Medicine Act 1960 medical laboratory scientific officers, physiotherapists and radiographers are the largest groups, constituting in all about three-quarters of those registered pursuant to the Act.

Professionalisation carries with it additions of both status and responsibility. The status of professions supplementary to medicine, as provided for in the 1960 Act and in orders made under the Act, is enhanced by virtue of a statutory framework. State registration has been described[2] as 'a sign of professional maturity'. It is an indication to the world at large that the professions which are included within the statutory framework are able to 'regulate themselves for the protection of their patients'.

A statutory registration system adds not only this element of status, conditioning as it does both relations with other professions as well as relations with patients or clients who are served by the professions supplementary to medicine. It also carries with it connotations of proper qualifications and proper conduct. It is the function and the duty of investigating and disciplinary bodies to maintain high standards of conduct and to mark lapses with a professional penalty. But the registering bodies themselves may also be concerned with questions of good conduct and good character before registration or renewal of registration. Such questions are raised in the following chapter which discusses professional discipline under the Act and its orders in some detail.

Suffice it to say for present purposes that the three functions of maintaining a register, exercising a disciplinary function in relation to practitioners entered on the register, and the general supervision of standards and institutions of education in their relevant specialist fields, are the principal responsibilities of the eight boards constituted under the provisions of the Professions Supplementary to Medicine Act 1960.

Relationship of the professions to medicine

As has been noted already the professions supplementary to medicine, included within the statutory framework established under the Act of 1960, are by no means exhaustive of professions and specialties, which in their own separate ways supplement and assist the medical treatment of patients. The present chapter is about the statutory framework and its constituent elements and functions, so it is necessary to concentrate attention on those professions which are represented by their respective boards in the statutory scheme of things. It should not be forgotten, however, that a very substantial number of the legal rules, regulations and principles to be examined in this book are of equal application to professions which maintain a similar function to those specifically discussed in connection with the structure created by the Professions Supplementary to Medicine Act 1960.

The eight professions included within the framework established under the 1960 Act are all in their own way closely connected to and involved with medical practice. The setting up of a statutory structure side by side with a similar structure in respect of the practice of medicine creates an important forum of negotiation. In particular it provides an established context within which the particular relations and respective responsibilities of the two professional groups can be constantly assessed. It is a context in which these relations and responsibilities can be suitably negotiated and renegotiated.

Questions whether chiropodists should be able to perform minor foot surgery, whether medical laboratory scientific officers should perform pregnancy tests in the absence of a reference from or to a medical practitioner, and whether these professionals should be appointed to manage pathology laboratories, are all questions which have been the subject of recent inquiry and debate. The principle involved in each case concerns the nature and ambit of the professional role, and the propriety and acceptability of that role as judged from the point of view of others, including especially members of the medical profession.

SCOPE OF PROFESSIONAL PRACTICE

It is appropriate to consider briefly the 'scope rules' by reference to which the boards of the professions supplementary to medicine outline and limit the 'territory' of registered practitioners' functions and responsibilities. Not surprisingly, the scope rules adopted by each of the eight statutory boards are interwoven with the definition of behaviour or practice which might constitute 'infamous conduct' (serious professional misconduct). More detailed attention to the misconduct aspects of the boards' rules is therefore reserved for the following chapter, in which the subject of discipline as such is examined.

The general theme of the scope rules adopted by each of the eight registered professions supplementary to medicine is that, except in the case of chiropody, patients are usually referred by a doctor. Furthermore certain prohibitions are issued against claims to be able to diagnose and treat illness. It is worth looking briefly at the scope rules of each of the eight professions in order to note similarities and differences in the principles adopted.

In the case of orthoptists, radiographers and remedial gymnasts the respective boards for those professions specifically in their rules prohibit practitioners from undertaking treatment in the absence of a referral by a medical practitioner. The Physiotherapists Board says: 'No physiotherapist should treat a patient unless that patient has been referred to him/her by a registered medical or dental practitioner, except in an emergency or for some other exceptional reason, or unless he/she has direct access to the patient's doctor'. The scope for physiotherapists is therefore widened in these respects. Similar instructions are given to occupational therapists, though in their case the board does not refer to cases of emergency, as the respective objectives of the relevant therapy differ.

Dietitians are instructed by their board that they shall not *habitually* treat any patient therapeutically without instructions given by a registered medical or dental practitioner. The Disciplinary Committee of the Dietitians Board would not regard the giving of general nutritional and dietary advice to groups as a breach of this provision.

Medical laboratory scientific officers are told by the Medical Laboratory Technicians Board that no registered practitioner should 'knowingly accept, obtain, assist in obtaining or report on any specimen for the purpose of the diagnosis and/or treatment of disease, or make any investigation for those purposes unless the diagnosis and/or treatment are to be performed by a registered medical, dental or veterinary practitioner'. This rule is not, explains an addendum to the board's statement, to be construed as preventing registered medical laboratory scientific officers from conducting pregnancy tests independently. But the board advises them when so doing to include with their report on the test a recommendation that the patient report the results to her doctor or, if the patient is willing, to report them directly to the doctor.

Further restrictions are imposed by the scope rules on the scope of acceptable registered professional conduct. Registered radiographers are instructed not to hold themselves out as persons who by training or experience are professionally qualified to diagnose or treat injury or disease. Registered remedial gymnasts are instructed not to undertake or give or accept responsibility for any form of treatment in which they are not trained and do not hold a recognised qualification. Registered physiotherapists are also instructed, by their board, to confine themselves to treatment in those forms of physiotherapy in which they have been trained. Registered medical laboratory scientific officers should not hold themselves out as persons who, by training or experience, are professionally qualified to diagnose or treat disease in man or animal.

The relationships between the medical profession and professions supplementary to it are maintained not only by inter-professional discussion, by scope rules and by practical relations in day-to-day patient care and treatment. The statutory framework established by the 1960 Act provides also for the inclusion of medical nominees as members of the board for each profession represented on the Council for Professions Supplementary to Medicine. It is now appropriate to examine the statutory structure in detail, looking first at the framework of the Council and its boards.

THE PROFESSIONS SUPPLEMENTARY TO MEDICINE ACT 1960

The process of professionalisation in professions supplementary to medicine began well before the enactment of the statute of 1960. In 1936 the British Medical Association, together with some of the 'auxiliary' professions as they were then called, established a body with the title Board of Registration of Medical Auxiliaries. It was the function of this body to maintain a voluntary register for workers who provided patient services under the supervision of doctors.

That board came in time to represent chiropodists, opticians, physiotherapists, radiographers and almoners, as well as technicians in operating theatres, audiology and venereology. Registration with the Board was conditional on one of a variety of qualifications, which were normally the qualifications administered and awarded by the respective professional institutions. 'The Board was effectively under the wing of the BMA, which not only subsidised its staff and accommodation but also kept a fatherly eye on the various groups and tried to help improve their conditions, status and pay.'[3]

As time went on and practice developed, the term 'auxiliary' became outmoded as a description of the various specialist paramedical contributions which were being made by these groups. Pressure began to rise for the establishment of a single body to administer statutory registration for the paramedical professions and to consider education and training.

One step in this direction was taken in 1954 by the creation of the National Health Service (Medical Auxiliaries) Regulations.[4] But it was not until 1960 that a full-blown statute was passed to govern such paramedical professions as it then comprised, and which were thenceforth statutorily referred to as 'professions supplementary to medicine'.

The Professions Supplementary to Medicine Act 1960 establishes a framework comprising a Council and eight separate registration boards. The Council and the boards are related to each other by way of federation, in which each registration board (one for each of the professions represented on the Council) retains a separate existence and a substantial degree of autonomy, and in which the Council for Professions Supplementary to Medicine maintains a general co-ordinating and supervisory role.

The eight boards in this federal arrangement represent the following professions: chiropodists, dietitians, occupational therapists, orthoptists, physiotherapists, radiographers, remedial gymnasts and medical laboratory scientific officers. Speech therapists were included in the original discussions, but decided at a late stage in the negotiations not to go forward into the scheme which was created by the 1960 Act. The profession of orthoptists joined the statutory scheme in 1966 by way of the Professions Supplementary to Medicine (Orthoptists Board) Order of Council[5] which came into operation on 16 August 1966.

The Council and the Boards

The Council for Professions Supplementary to Medicine (CPSM) consists of a membership of 23. The chairmen of the eight registration boards are always elected as members of the CPSM, although the Act itself (Sched. 1, para. 1(1)(c)) simply refers to 'persons . . . of whom one shall be appointed by each of the boards established under this Act from among the representative members of that board'. These eight board representatives are matched by eight medical representatives, and the Act provides for a further seven Council members all of whom shall be laymen (Sched. 1, paras. 1(1)(a), 1(1)(b)).

The CPSM has the general function of co-ordinating and supervising the activities of the statutory boards which the Act also establishes. And it is given the job of seeing that high standards of professional education and training, and high standards of professional conduct, are maintained among the members of the eight represented professions (ss.1(1), 1(2)).

In performing its co-ordinating and supervisory function in relation to the eight boards, the CPSM has statutory responsibilities which include: making to each board, or inviting the board to make to the Council, proposals as to the activities to be carried on by the board or other boards; recommending a board to carry on such activities, or to limit its activities in such a manner, as the Council considers appropriate after consultation with the board on such proposals; concerning itself with matters which appear to the Council to be of special interest to any two or more of the boards, and by giving the boards such advice as it thinks fit in this connection; and exercising its powers under the Act in such a way as the Council considers most conducive to the satisfactory performance by each board of the board's functions under the Act (s.1(3)). The particular functions which are carried out by the boards include principally registration, the setting of educational standards, and the maintenance of discipline.

The CPSM may appoint committees to carry out such of its functions as it may decide are best done in such a way or which merit such treatment. The Council may also make standing orders to regulate both its own proceedings and those of any committee which it may establish.

A further important statutory function of the CPSM relates to the possible alterations to the structure of the Council and the number of professions supplementary to medicine which are represented on it in the form of individual boards. If the CPSM considers it appropriate, after consulting any existing board or boards which appear to be concerned, that certain changes should be made then it has a duty to make an appropriate recommendation to the Privy Council.

The principal such change would be that the provision of the Professions Supplementary to Medicine Act 1960 should be extended to include a profession which appears to the CPSM to be a 'profession supplementary to medicine' but which is not presently included under the Act, that is, it has not got a Board as defined under the Act and is not represented on the CPSM. The only addition which has so far been made to the statutory structure since the 1960 Act came into force has been the addition of the profession of orthoptics in 1966.

A converse duty is also imposed on the CPSM if, having regard to the activities usually carried on by persons practising one of the professions covered by the Act, a recommendation appears to be necessary that the Act should cease to extend to that profession. Power also exists for the Privy Council to act on a recommendation from the CPSM that the functions of an individual board may be altered; and in the event of an amalgamation or proposed amalgamation of a profession covered by the Act with another profession (whether or not so covered), to amalgamate the professions concerned under a single board with an appropriate name.

The statutory framework established by the 1960 Act provides for up to 12 boards within the CPSM. This certainly appears to be sufficient for forseeable purposes. The boards now represented on the Council under the provisions of the Act are: the Chiropodists Board, the Dietitians Board, the Medical Laboratory Technicians Board, the Occupational Therapists Board, the Orthoptists Board, the Physiotherapists Board, the Radiographers Board and the Remedial Gymnasts Board.

Membership of each of the boards varies in number between 11 (orthoptists, chiropodists and remedial gymnasts) and 17 (occupational therapists and physiotherapists). The Dietitians Board has 15 members and the boards for medical laboratory technicians and radiographers each have 13 members.

The functions of the boards are expressed in general terms by section 1(2) of the 1960 Act to be those of 'promoting high standards of professional education and professional conduct among members of the relevant profession'. The professional institutions themselves, such as the Chartered Society of Physiotherapy (CSP), are the examining bodies. The boards, in this example the Physiotherapists Board, are there to maintain and recommend standards rather than to administer the examinations themselves. The Council too, in its co-ordinating and supervisory capacity, has also played a part in policies and standards affecting education and training for the professions supplementary to medicine. Certain educational recommendations were made in the 1980 CPSM document *PSM Registration and Self-Regulation: Future Requirements and Opportunities* (the recommendations on registration and discipline are discussed separately, below). And in its education report *The Next Decade* a recommendation was made for an investigation into the need for degree level education for each of the professions.

It is the duty of each of the boards to prepare and maintain a register of names, addresses and qualifications of all persons who are entitled in accordance with the provisions of the Act to be registered by the board and who apply for registration in the appropriate manner. A person is entitled to be registered by a board if the board is satisfied that he has attended a course of training approved by the board under the Act, and that the course was given in whole or in part at an approved institution; and that the applicant for registration is indeed qualified.

Registration and use of title

A person who has registered or renewed registration with one of the eight boards is entitled to use the title which such registration entails. For instance, a chiropodist so registered may use the title 'state registered chiropodist' and a physiotherapist the title 'state registered physiotherapist', and so on, for the other professions supplementary to medicine.

Criminal offences are created by the 1960 Act in respect of improper use of such titles, as well as in respect of the fraudulent obtaining of registrations. The protection given by the Act to registered title is found in section 6(2), which provides: 'Any person who (a) takes or uses alone or in conjunction with any other words, the title state registered chiropodist, state chiropodist or registered chiropodist (and similarly as respects the other professions . . .) when his name is not on the register established under this Act in respect of that profession; or (b) takes or uses any name, title, addition or description falsely implying, or otherwise pretends, that his name is on a register established under this Act, shall be liable on summary conviction to a fine not exceeding fifty pounds and, in the case of a second or subsequent conviction, to a fine not exceeding one hundred pounds.' Summary conviction means in a trial before magistrates in the absence of a jury.

The effect of the Criminal Justice Act 1982, sections 35–46 was to increase these maximum fines to £100 and £200 respectively. The maximum amounts still appear relatively low. It is interesting to compare the maximum fine in the case of professions supplementary to medicine with the fine which can be imposed for the corresponding offence relating to the use of a medical title. Any person who wilfully and falsely pretends to be registered under any provision of the Medical Act 1956 is liable to a fine of up to £500.

An offence in respect of the actual inclusion of a person's name on one of the professional registers is provided for in section 7 of the Professions Supplementary to Medicine Act 1960, which reads: 'If a person procures or attempts to procure the entry of any name on a register established under this Act by wilfully making or producing or causing to be made or produced, either verbally or in writing, any declaration, certificate or representation which he knows to be false or fraudulent, he shall be liable on summary conviction to a fine not exceeding one hundred pounds.'

Protection of title

Any person who is qualified and registered with one of the eight boards for professions supplementary to medicine may use the title 'state registered', or just 'state' or 'registered', followed by the name of the particular professional occupation. The offence in relation to title indicated above consists in the pretence or false use of such a title. This is as far as the Act goes in relation to the protection of statutory title.

A physiotherapist, therefore, who is not registered under the 1960 Act with the Physiotherapists Board may still call himself or herself a physiotherapist. And if such a person is a member of the professional society, the Chartered Society of Physiotherapy, he or she may use the description 'chartered physiotherapist'.

There is one way in which registered title pertaining to the professions supplementary to medicine receives more than this relatively slight protection. The National Health Service (Professions Supplementary to Medicine) Regulations 1974[6] provide that no member of the professions supplementary to medicine so mentioned in the 1960 Act may be employed as an officer of a regional, district or special health authority unless he or she is registered under the Act in respect of the profession appropriate to the work for which he or she is employed.

Thus, in the example of the unregistered physiotherapist given above, such a person could use the title 'physiotherapist' or call himself a chartered physiotherapist if a member of the CSP, but could not be employed in National Health Service work. There would be nothing to prevent an unregistered person from being employed in the independent health care sector, for the independent sector lies outside the ambit of these regulations. Private practice as a physiotherapist, or in other professions supplementary to medicine, is also unaffected by the regulations and by the 1960 Act except in so far as use of title bestowed by the Act is concerned.

The relatively weak protection given to title under the statutory arrangements just described has been criticised, and it has been identified as a source of problems. On the one hand statutory registration demonstrates to the public who may use the service offered a high degree of competence in the particular person whose professional services are sought and used. On the other hand there are a great many unregistered practitioners and professionals of high calibre and expertise who are engaged in private practice as well as in the public service and institutions outside the National Health Service.

Unregistered practice can be seen as a major problem in chiropody[7] and a further step known as 'closure' of the profession (the term is explained below) has frequently been urged in the case of chiropody, in which there is a very large measure of private practice. The CPSM has also identified the weakness of existing protection of title. In the report of a working party published in 1980 it said: 'Avoidance of registration requirements in fringe employment like prison hospitals, university medical school laboratories, and possibly among NHS contractors, as well as in private practice, makes the existing requirement even more anomalous'.[8]

It could be seen as an anomaly in itself that while the 1974 NHS (Professions Supplementary to Medicine) Regulations prevent the employment of unregistered professionals by health authorities, their employment by NHS contractors, whose employees may be numerous, is not so affected.

Earlier it was said that such 'protection' as is given to registered professional title by the Professions Supplementary to Medicine Act 1960 is relatively weak. The protection is derived from improper use of the state registered titles to which those falling within the Act are entitled. But there are many who would deny that this really amounts to any protection of title at all.

Protection of title is usually taken to go beyond the protection, via the imposition of criminal penalties in the event of prohibited use, of titles such as 'state registered chiropodist'. Protection of title, in its more usual sense, involves a restriction on the very use of the professional title, such as 'physiotherapist' or 'chiropodist', to those professionals who are registered under the Act.

This form of protection of title would have the effect of pushing unregistered practitioners a considerable step further away from their professional colleagues who are registered. It would mean not only that an unregistered chiropodist could not lawfully use the title 'state registered chiropodist' but further that such a person would not call himself or herself a 'chiropodist' at all. Practice would have to be pursued under some other form of title. But *practice*, be it noted, would not in such a scheme be prohibited.

Protection of title in this form is also sometimes referred to as 'indicative closure'. The term 'closure' is explained below, and it is important not to confuse the protection of title just described with the *closure* of a *profession*. A DHSS consultative document published in December 1981[9] uses the term 'indicative closure' to refer to protection of title in the sense explained above. The 'indication' refers to the form in which the practitioner in question is described, or *indicated*. The 'closure' would, in such a scheme, be limited to a restriction on the way in which paramedical practitioners would be able to describe themselves or indicate themselves, in a directory of practitioners, for instance.

The consultative document refers on page 5 to indicative closure, or protection of title in the following terms: 'At the time of the Professions Supplementary to Medicine Act the hope was expressed that the standard of state registration would come to be so widely accepted as the one to look for in seeking treatment that the unregistered sector would wither away. In practice the public appear to have continued to make full use of the services of unregistered practitioners as well as of those who are registered, and the services by unregistered practitioners are meeting consumer demand and increasing consumer choice. Indicative closure would give the public the means of distinguishing between registered and unregistered practitioners but unlike functional closure it would not restrict the services available.'

Closure of the professions, or what the DHSS referred to in the passage just quoted as 'functional closure', is a further stage still and involves a complete closure of a profession to all those who do not have the benefit of state registration. The effect of complete closure would, in the example given earlier, have the effect that an unregistered physiotherapist would not even be allowed to practise as such. It would, to use the distinction drawn in the consultative document between indicative and functional closure, be a restriction (indeed a prohibition) on the very functions of the physiotherapist or whomever, and not just on what such practitioners could call themselves though still freely practising as such.

The DHSS consultative document produced a variety of arguments against functional closure. But it suggested that the common titles of the eight professions supplementary to medicine (together with the profession of speech therapy, which was originally to be included in the framework created by the 1960 Act) might be protected.

Other recommendations as to registration

The CPSM working party publication of 1980 makes a number of further recommendations in addition to proposals that there should be legal powers to protect title or even to close a profession.[10] These other recommendations include the proposal for a discretionary power to grant only provisional registration, subject to conditions of supervision or tests of competence as may be thought appropriate, to those who have for three years failed to renew their registration; and also to those who, in any period of the preceding five years, had been registered for only two of them.

A power is proposed in the case of any registrant continuously registered for five years or more to require evidence which will satisfy the board in question that he has continued to have such professional experience as will have maintained his competence. Failure to produce such evidence would lead to the need to pass, within two years, a test of satisfactory competence. Failure in such a test would lead to withdrawal of registration.

In the context of its discussion of protection of title and closure the DHSS consultative document also raised the possibility of a ‘tiered’ profession with a lower level of state enrolment for professionals with less training.

Speech therapists

It was noted earlier (p. 33) that an unregistered paramedical practitioner may not, owing to provisions made by regulations in 1974, be employed in the National Health Service. Speech therapists were not eventually included within the framework established by the Professions Supplementary to Medicine Act 1960. Nevertheless, a restriction on employment of speech therapists in the NHS was made and issued simultaneously with, and in very similar terms to, the restriction applicable to the eight professions within the Act.[11]

Instead of registration, however, which does not apply in the case of speech therapists, the regulation imposes certain other conditions. No person shall be employed by a health authority as a speech therapist unless he or she holds a certificate issued by the College of Speech Therapists. The certificate must state that the person in question attended a course of training, and passed an examination, approved by the Secretary of State.

REFERENCES

[1] *British Medical Journal* (1982), **284**, 680
[2] ibid.
[3] ibid.
[4] S.I. 1954 No. 55
[5] S.I. 1966 No. 990
[6] S.I. 1974 No. 494
[7] *British Medical Journal* article, above, (1)
[8] *PSM Registration and Self-Regulation: Future Requirements and Opportunities*, p. 4 (CPSM, April 1980)
[9] *Proposals for Statutory Protection of Professional Title under the Professions Supplementary to Medicine Act 1960 and Closure of the Speech Therapy Profession*, p. 3 (DHSS, December 1981)
[10] op. cit. p. 13
[11] S.I. 1974 No. 495

Chapter Three

PROFESSIONAL DISCIPLINE

An important effect of any system of statutory registration for a profession has already been noted. That is, that the public is thereby shown a guarantee of professional competence. State registration indicates an official, state recognition. To say this is not, of course, in any way to imply that unregistered members of any of the professions supplementary to medicine are less competent than their registered counterparts. It is simply to make the positive point that state registration constitutes a further, and official, mark of approval.

Registration with one of the boards of the professions supplementary to medicine includes the practitioner in a system which maintains standards of professional conduct and ensures basic standards of competence and of education when first registering. A further addition to the positive encouragement of such standards is a system by which discipline can be maintained, if necessary by way of sanctions in the event of breaches of professional standards or conduct. While the registration system is the mark of steps taken in the direction of high professional standards, disciplinary rules and principles are required in the event of lapses from such standards.

It is the duty of each board established by the Professions Supplementary to Medicine Act 1960 to set up a disciplinary system. The structure required by the Act comprises an investigating committee and a disciplinary committee for each of the boards. The investigating committee has the duty of conducting a preliminary investigation into any case in which it is alleged that a person registered by the particular board in question has conducted himself or herself in such a way as to become liable to removal from the register. It is up to the investigating committee to decide, following such investigation, whether the case should then be referred to the disciplinary committee of the board.

If a case is indeed referred by the investigating committee to the disciplinary committee it is the statutory duty of the disciplinary committee to consider and rule on the case.[1] A decision of the disciplinary committee to remove a person's name from the register does not, as was explained in Chapter 2, mean that the person cannot lawfully practise at all in his or her professional capacity; it simply means that such a person is disallowed, during the period in which the name is absent from the board's register, from using the title 'state registered'. The relatively weak protection (some would not call it protection at all) given to professional title would in practice leave a number of avenues open to the practitioner involved. The name of the profession could still be used, such as 'chiropodist' or 'physiotherapist'. And removal from the board's register could not prohibit the person in question from continuing to exercise the *function* of chiropodist, physiotherapist and so on, save that employment as such in the National Health Service would be ruled out on account of the 1974 regulations[2] which were mentioned in the previous chapter (p. 33).

The statutory effect of removal of a name from a board's register is given in section 9(5) of the Professions Supplementary to Medicine Act 1960, which provides that:

> A person whose name is removed from a register in pursuance of a direction of a disciplinary committee under this section shall not be entitled to be registered in that register again except in pursuance of a direction in that behalf given by the committee on the application of that person; and a direction under this section for the removal of a person's name from the register may prohibit an application under this subsection by that person until the expiration of such period from the date of the direction (and where he has duly made such an application, from the date of his last application) as may be specified in the direction.

In other words, a person whose name has been removed from a register must take the positive step of applying to have it restored. And the disciplinary committee has the power to prohibit the reinstatement of the person in question until a specified period has elapsed. In this way the committee may mark the gravity of a particular offence or breach of professional standards.

No person who has acted as a member of the investigating committee in a particular case is allowed to be a member also of the disciplinary committee to which that case is referred. In this way the disciplinary rules secure the observance of natural justice and ensure fairness in the structure of the bodies who have jurisdiction to affect individual rights in such a significant way.[3]

The procedure of a disciplinary committee of a board established under the 1960 Act is governed by the Professions Supplementary to Medicine (Disciplinary Committees) (Procedure) Rules Order of Council made in 1964.[4] These rules provide for the appointment of a chairman, notice of inquiry in cases relating to conduct and cases which involve an allegation of a criminal conviction, postponement or cancellation of an inquiry, access to necessary and relevant documents, the reading of the charge, proof of the facts which are alleged in the charge, evidence, voting, representation and certain other procedural matters including the taking of shorthand notes during the proceedings.

For the purpose of any proceedings before it a disciplinary committee has the power to administer oaths. Any party to the disciplinary proceedings may use the writs of subpoena (for the purpose of compelling the attendance of witnesses) and of *duces tecum* (for the purpose of compelling the production of documents in evidence).

In order for the disciplinary committee to have advice relating to questions of law which may arise before it there must in all disciplinary proceedings be a legal assessor to the committee. The legal assessor must be a barrister, advocate or solicitor of not less than 10 years' standing. The particular functions of legal assessors are set out in the Professions Supplementary to Medicine (Disciplinary Proceedings) Legal Assessor Rules made in 1964.[5] The legal assessor must immediately inform the disciplinary committee of any irregularity in the conduct of the proceedings which becomes known to him, and he must advise the committee when he considers that a mistake of law would be made in the absence of his advice and intervention to the contrary.

Where an assessor advises a disciplinary committee on any question of law relating to evidence, procedure or other matters specified in the disciplinary rules, he must do so in the presence of every party, or person representing a party, to the proceedings who has appeared at the proceedings. And if the assessor's legal advice is tendered while the disciplinary committee is deliberating in private, every party or representative must be informed of the advice tendered by the assessor. This is a further way in which the disciplinary rules ensure not only that justice is done but is also seen to be done.

In a case in which the disciplinary committee of a board finds the charge against the practitioner in question proved and directs that the name of that person be removed from the board's register, the practitioner has a statutory right of appeal to the Privy Council. The notice of the committee's direction to remove the name from the register must be served on that person. An appeal may be made at any time within 28 days from the date of the service upon him of notice of that direction.[6]

The appeal, being to the Privy Council, is made by way of a 'petition' to appeal. The petition must give a succinct statement of the principal stages in the proceedings leading up to the appeal. It must not itself, however, contain argumentative matter, nor should it discuss the merits of the case. Though the appeal is in theory a rehearing of the case against the petitioner (the appellant), the witnesses are not heard again and the evidence is not gone over again. It has been pointed out[7] that these features of a petition against erasure to the Privy Council place a heavy burden on a practitioner who appeals on the ground that the evidence alone renders the decision of the disciplinary committee unsatisfactory.

On the question of a 'rehearing' of the case against the practitioner whose name has been removed from a board's register, further instructive guidance can be had from the words of Lord Hailsham, the Lord Chancellor, in a case which in fact involved disciplinary proceedings in the medical profession but which is equally applicable to appeals from proceedings in the context of professions supplementary to medicine:

> Beyond a bare statement of its findings of fact, the disciplinary committee does not in general give reasons for its decision as in the case of a trial in the High Court . . . It follows from this that the only circumstances in which an appellate court can reverse a view of the facts taken by the disciplinary committee would be a case where, on examination, it would appear that the committee had misread the evidence to such an extent that they were not entitled to make a finding in the state of the evidence presented before them.[8]

THE GROUNDS FOR DISCIPLINARY ACTION

The Professions Supplementary to Medicine Act 1960 is fairly terse as to the reasons for which a board's disciplinary committee may consider the step of removing the name of a practitioner from the relevant register. Section 9 of the Act gives three separate reasons for which a name may be so removed.

First, the step may be taken where a person whose name is included on the register of a board is convicted by any court in the United Kingdom of a criminal offence which, in the opinion of the disciplinary committee set up by the board, renders that person unfit to be registered.

Second, striking off the register may be appropriate where such a person is judged by the disciplinary committee to be guilty of 'infamous conduct' in any professional respect. And, thirdly, where the disciplinary committee finds that the name of such a person has in fact been fraudulently entered on the register maintained by the board.

When the disciplinary committee directs that a person's name be removed from the register it has a legal duty to cause notice of the direction to be served on the person concerned. It should be noted that the three alternative grounds of jurisdiction to remove a name from the board's register which were given above do no more than confer upon a disciplinary committee the legal power to remove a practitioner's name from the register of the relevant board 'if it thinks fit' to do so. The committee has a discretion in the matter, and there is no legal duty to strike off if the committee chooses not to take that step. The fact that the Act leaves a disciplinary committee's discretion in this form has given grounds for suggestions for reform in certain respects which are discussed below.

Each one of the grounds for which there is jurisdiction to remove a name from the register merits closer and more detailed examination. The following elaboration of the grounds of jurisdiction takes them in the order in which they were introduced above.

Conviction of a criminal offence

We take first the jurisdiction to remove from the register the name of a practitioner who has been convicted of a criminal offence in the United Kingdom. It might be mentioned in passing that a conviction for a criminal offence imposed outside the United Kingdom, though not within this particular ground of jurisdiction, might in appropriate circumstances be relevant to the separate ground of jurisdiction based on so-called 'infamous conduct', which is discussed in the following section of this chapter. The purpose of making a criminal conviction ground for removing the name of a practitioner from the register of the board in question may be explained by reference to the words of Lord Diplock, the then senior Law Lord, in a case involving proceedings on this ground which had been determined by the General Dental Council. The matter of principle is equally applicable to the case of professions supplementary to medicine:

> The purpose of disciplinary proceedings against a [practitioner] who has been convicted of a criminal offence by a court of law is not to punish him a second time for the same offence, but to protect the public who may come to him as patients and to maintain the high standards and good reputation of an honourable profession.[9]

The discretion of the disciplinary committee of the relevant board is abundantly necessary under this head of jurisdiction. For it is not every criminal conviction which could conceivably lead to a consideration of the possibility of removal from the register. Parking and certain minor motoring and other technical offences are clearly not so heinous that they would remotely justify erasure from the register. But offences involving dishonesty and fraud would be very likely to do so, as also would convictions for offences involving physical injury or harm to the person. Depending on the particular circumstances in which such an offence had been committed the element, mentioned earlier, of the 'protection of the public who may come as patients' may well be found to be present in a case before the disciplinary committee.

Of course, certain criminal convictions may still be a very long way from meriting removal from the register as an additional 'protection'. As to the gravity of the offence of which the practitioner in question has been convicted, the further words of Lord Diplock in the case mentioned above are instructive. He said that

> it would be the duty of the disciplinary committee, before deciding to inflict the only and draconian penalty which lies within their power, to satisfy themselves that the offence of which the [practitioner] had been convicted was of so grave a

> character as to show that he was unfitted to continue to practise his profession.

The 'draconian' penalty of erasure of the practitioner's name from the register, mentioned by Lord Diplock in a case which in fact concerned proceedings before the General Dental Council, is found also in the context of disciplinary proceedings relating to the professions supplementary to medicine. The report of the CPSM working party published in 1980 identified the requirement for powers of disciplinary committees not only to remove a name from the register but also to suspend registration for a specified period. This power now exists in the case of medical practitioners. Such a power of suspension from the register would, the CPSM suggested, be coupled with the reinstatement of the practitioner in question under given conditions of practice, supervision and/or medical advice, or subject to such other conditions as the disciplinary committee might consider appropriate.

A further apparent deficiency in the present system of discipline based on the practitioner's commission of a criminal offence is this. It appears from the Act[10] that ground for removal of a person's name from the register kept by a board is based only on the commission of a relevant offence subsequent to registration and not before it. Given the words of Lord Diplock quoted above, the conditions under which a convicted person might justifiably be debarred from professional registered practice are such that this limitation in point of time on a disciplinary committee's jurisdiction is inappropriate.

The CPSM working party therefore said this:

> Under present powers Boards have no jurisdiction over misconduct or criminal offences committed either before initial registration or while the registrant is temporarily removed for non-payment of the annual fee during periods when presumably he is not working for the NHS.[11] This anomaly should be corrected by a requirement for registrants to have been of good character or alternatively free from specified convictions during periods prior to first registration or annual renewal.[12]

Such a requirement is probably more easily suggested than it is capable of being made in specific practical terms. For the ruling of a disciplinary committee in the light of the nature and gravity of the particular offence or offences complained of is necessarily *ex post facto*, or after the event and with the wisdom of hindsight, as well as the foresight of future protection. Creating conditions in advance tends to be an open-ended procedure and as such not at all easy.

Serious professional misconduct

The second of the three grounds on the basis of which the 1960 Act empowers the disciplinary committees of boards to consider removal of a name from the register is where the practitioner in question has been judged 'guilty of infamous conduct in any professional respect' by the committee. In the present discussion the expression 'serious professional misconduct' is used (except in the case of specific reference to the 1960 Act) in preference to the relatively outmoded 'infamous conduct in any professional respect'. The more modern expression has indeed been substituted in corresponding disciplinary provisions affecting the medical profession, in a statute enacted some years after the Professions Supplementary to Medicine Act was passed.[13]

The Professions Supplementary to Medicine Act provides for the matter of 'infamous conduct' in the following broad terms:

> It shall be the duty of each disciplinary committee to prepare and from time to time revise, in consultation with its board and the Council, a statement as to the kind of conduct which the committee considers to be infamous conduct in a professional respect, and the board shall send by post to each registered member of the relevant profession, at his address on the register, a copy of the statement as for the time being revised; but the fact that any matters are not mentioned in such a statement shall not preclude the disciplinary committee from judging a person to be guilty of infamous conduct in a professional respect by reference to such matters.[14]

Guidance as to the practical significance and meaning of 'serious professional misconduct' may be derived by reference to medical and dental cases which have necessitated judicial comment because they have gone on appeal from the disciplinary committees concerned to the Privy Council. As to the broad generality of the expression, Lord Guest said in a case which came before the Privy Council in 1970:

> There are no closed categories of infamous conduct and in every case it must be a question for the committee to decide first whether the facts alleged in the charge have been proved and second whether the appellant was in relation to those facts guilty of infamous conduct in a professional respect.[15]

As to what will be considered to be serious professional misconduct, the opinion of professional colleagues is most important. Conduct which professional opinion of good standing and repute would consider to be serious professional misconduct is most likely to be judged as such in a disciplinary committee. Where misconduct in matters of record-keeping is concerned, peer group opinion that a practitioner has been careless will not normally be sufficient to condemn him. There must in general be shown to be also an element of fraud or dishonesty, or such reckless disregard of professional duty as may reasonably be equated with dishonesty.[16] In one case a medical practitioner was judged guilty of serious professional misconduct when he gained access to a family professionally and later entered into an improper association with the wife, even though she had ceased to be his patient before the association began.[17]

In each of these cases, subject to any appropriate variation to suit likely factual conditions, the jurisdiction in respect of serious professional misconduct could be expected to be exercised in the same way and on the same grounds in the case of an offending member of a profession supplementary to medicine.

Statements by the Disciplinary Committees

It would take too long to give a full account here of conduct which the disciplinary committees of the eight boards have pronounced *in advance* to be serious professional misconduct. A common feature, however, is a restriction or sometimes a prohibition on advertising. On registered remedial gymnasts, for instance, a total prohibition is imposed on advertising or canvassing, direct or indirect. Direct or indirect canvassing are similarly prohibited for registered physiotherapists. But their board states that it would not regard it as a breach of the restriction on advertising for a physiotherapist to write to registered medical or dental practitioners in order to draw attention to the registered physiotherapist's name, address, qualifications and to the fact that his or her services as a physiotherapist are available. Indeed, such information, properly used, tends to the advantage and furtherance of patient care by the co-operating professions.

Owing to the investigatory nature of their professional function, registered radiographers and medical laboratory scientific officers both share the following instruction from their respective boards. No registered member of either of those professions should 'Knowingly disclose to any patient, or to any other unauthorised person, the result of any investigations or any other information of a personal or confidential nature gained in the course of practice of his/her profession.'

The underlying objective of these and a variety of other prohibitions and restrictions appropriate to the particular professions is the dual one of protecting the probity of the profession and protecting the health and safety of the patient. In addition to the statements of 'infamous conduct' (serious professional misconduct) each board issues an introductory statement designed to explain these dual objectives to registered members. A revised form of this introduction was agreed upon in the early part of 1983 and the required issue to members commenced shortly afterwards. Referring to section 9(6) of the Professions Supplementary to Medicine Act 1960, which is the legal provision requiring the issuing of such statements by the disciplinary committees of the eight boards, the standard form of introduction now includes the following paragraphs which elaborate on the duality of objectives mentioned above:

> In considering the establishment of such a code of conduct for the profession the Committee has considered the underlying principle of such a self-imposed code of ethics which is intended to establish the relationship between the professional person and those to whom he or she has a professional responsibility and to resolve the conflicts which arise between the interests of patients and the professional person or the community at large. The adoption of such a code of discipline which involves establishing ethical rules and restrictions beyond those required of the ordinary citizen by law, sometimes to the personal disadvantage of the professional person, is designed to establish the probity and competence of the profession in the eyes of the public.

Specifically in relation to the protection of the patient the standard introduction adds:

> The Committee wishes to emphasise that while the statement contains a number of specific instances it is impossible to compile a complete list of conduct which may at some time be regarded by the Committee as infamous, and registrants are reminded that the Act provides that the fact that any matters are not mentioned in the statement will not preclude the Committee from judging a person to be guilty of infamous conduct in a professional respect by reference to such matters. The Committee will have regard to the underlying principle referred to above and to the duty upon a member of the profession to have proper regard for the welfare of a patient so that the health or safety of the patient is not endangered.

In 1983, amid some controversy between the CPSM and individual professions, a new common first clause was introduced into the statements of infamous conduct. No practitioner should:

> By any act or omission do anything or cause anything to be done which he or she has reasonable ground for believing is likely either to endanger or affect adversely in a substantial way the health or safety of a patient or patients.

While this new addition owes its origin to debates surrounding participation in the long drawn out strike in the National Health Service during 1982, the statements make a clear separation between participation in industrial action as such, and action likely to harm patients. This separation of issues is effected by the following footnote to the common form of clause in the statements issued by the eight boards:

> The question of the relationship between the requirements of the statements and action taken in an industrial dispute has been raised on a number of occasions. It would not be proper for a Disciplinary Committee to be involved in the merits of any industrial dispute concerning registrants and their employers and the participation by registrants in industrial action would not be regarded as within the statement of conduct.
>
> The statement of conduct is concerned only with infamous conduct in a professional respect; the principles of conduct against which that will be judged are set out in the introduction to and the contents of the statement. The Disciplinary Committee will consider any allegation referred to them irrespective of whether or not the conduct complained of has arisen in the course of industrial action, or in any other circumstances.

Fraudulent entry on the register

The third and final ground for the removal of a person's name from the register kept by a board relates to fraudulent entry on the board's register. It was noted in the previous chapter that any person who procures or attempts to procure the entry of any name on a register established under the 1960 Act by wilfully making any declarations or representation which he knows to be false or fraudulent is liable on summary conviction to a fine of up to £100. If the disciplinary committee is satisfied that the name of such a person has been fraudulently entered on the register, the name may be directed to be removed from the register.

OPPORTUNITIES FOR CHANGE

In the report of its working party published in April 1980 the Council for Professions Supplementary to Medicine noted the responses from professional institutions and ministries to questions raised by it for discussion on the existing arrangements for discipline.[18]

While the existence of eight separate disciplinary arrangements is in a way inept and cumbersome, opinion was found to be divided on a proposal for a joint disciplinary function. Although the boards of the smaller professions might thereby be deprived of practical experience in disciplinary matters, the 1980 working paper noted the case for leaving arrangements as they were. Certainly, the autonomy of each of the eight registering professions would thereby be left unaffected.

As the law stands,[19] the name of a registrant convicted of fraudulent entry to the register can only be removed following a hearing by the disciplinary committee of the relevant board. The CPSM recommends that the law be changed to the effect that such conviction should carry with it automatic erasure without a requirement of a hearing by a disciplinary committee. Furthermore, proceedings must be instituted in cases of fraudulent entry within six months of the commission of the fraud,[20] a period which may, the CPSM notes, be too short always to permit detection. The 1980 working party report accordingly recommended that the time limit should be eliminated in order to avoid this problem. Fraudulent entries could then be proceeded against at any time, and further protection therefore given to the register and to those entered on it.

The CPSM's recommendation that existing disciplinary committees as at present constituted should have powers not only to remove a name from the board's register (a power given to them by the Act and by orders made under it) but also to order the suspension of a practitioner from the register was noted earlier. The draconian nature of the powers provided for in the Act was indicated, and the possibility of an alternative, lesser sanction was raised. The recommendation by the CPSM that intending registrants should be required by a board to be of good character, a matter also affecting entry to the register, was noted earlier in the present chapter as a matter related to criminal convictions following registration as a cause for removal of a person's name from the register. All these disciplinary powers could be exercised by disciplinary committees as constituted under the Professions Supplementary to Medicine Act 1960.

A recommendation of a different order was made in the same

CPSM report when the desirability of a committee to deal with health matters was discussed. A medical cases committee was recommended to be set up with a power to suspend registration and/or to restrict practice subject to certain conditions. The Council noted that while the statutory provisions in the 1960 Act allow for the regulation of fitness to practise on grounds of misconduct, they do not allow for regulation or restriction of practice on grounds of physical or mental ill-health.

A sad case came before the disciplinary committee of the Occupational Therapists Board involving a criminal conviction in which the magistrates had ordered probation with a view to psychiatric treatment. It was with the greatest regret that the Occupational Therapists Board had to exercise the draconian power of erasure of the name of the registrant. Proposals initiated by the Occupational Therapists Board for a change in the disciplinary rules, though supported by all the boards and by the Council, were said by the Privy Council to be *ultra vires*. That is to say, the alternative action suggested was outside the bounds of the statutory powers. Ironically, of all the boards it is only the Occupational Therapists Board which customarily includes a psychiatrist.

In making the recommendation for formal procedures affecting practice on health grounds the CPSM said:

> A medical cases committee would appear to be a necessity, and in view of the requirement for specialised personnel who would be required to accumulate as much experience as there was available, it would seem appropriate for this to operate on a joint basis as a Council committee with professional assessors from the relevant board.[21]

While professional misconduct in its nature tends to involve the particular practices and ethical standards peculiar to the individual professions supplementary to medicine, the same is not necessarily true in cases where professional competence may be adversely affected by the physical or mental health of a practitioner. Some reasons for a board's consideration, through its committees, of professional conduct could involve both disciplinary and health grounds. In cases in which professional competence to practise, for instance, was alleged to be affected by drug abuse, procedures would be necessary for referral as between the disciplinary committee of an individual board and the proposed joint medical cases committee.

The powers of such a proposed medical cases committee would

probably be limited to suspension of registration for short fixed periods, subject to review at the end of the period. A power might also be introduced to impose conditions, including supervision, on the professional practice of the individual concerned.

REFERENCES

[1] Professions Supplementary to Medicine Act 1960, s.8(1)(b)
[2] S.I. 1974 No. 494
[3] 1960 Act, Schedule 2, para. 1(2)
[4] S.I. 1964 No. 1203
[5] S.I. 1964 No. 951
[6] Judicial Committee (Professions Supplementary to Medicine Rules) Order 1964, S.I. 1964 No. 1001
[7] Lord Hailsham in *Libman v. General Medical Council* [1972] (see 8 below)
[8] *Libman v. General Medical Council* [1972] 1 All E.R. 798, p. 800
[9] *Ziderman v. General Dental Council* [1976] 2 All E.R. 334, p. 336
[10] 1960 Act, s.9(1)(a)
[11] NHS (Professions Supplementary to Medicine) Regulations 1974, S.I. 1974 No. 494; see also Chapter 2 p. 33, above
[12] *PSM Registration and Self-Regulation: Future Requirements and Opportunities* (CPSM, April 1980) p. 15
[13] Medical Act 1969, s.13(2)(a)
[14] 1960 Act, s.9(6)
[15] Per Lord Guest in *Sloan v. General Medical Council* [1970] 2 All E.R. 686, p. 688
[16] *Felix v. General Dental Council* [1960] 2 All E.R. 391
[17] *De Gregory v. General Medical Council* [1961] A.C. 957
[18] op. cit., Chapter 3
[19] 1960 Act, s.9(1)(c)
[20] CPSM op. cit., Chapter 3 p. 15
[21] op. cit. p. 17

Chapter Four

EMPLOYMENT

WHO IS AN EMPLOYEE?

An essential distinction to be drawn in relation to both aspects of this chapter is that which exists between an employee and what the law calls an independent contractor. An employee is, by definition, employed, while an independent contractor is not employed as such but is engaged. Put differently, a distinction is drawn between a contract of employment, which is a contract of service, and a contract for services under which a contractor is engaged.

The use of words is no mere verbal difference, for an important distinction in substance exists between a contract of service and a contract for services. An employee is in the service of an employer, while an independent contractor is not. The contractor may, of course, be employed by some other employer, and may for the purposes of the question in issue be rendering services to, but not actually in the service of, the person for whom the contractor is doing a job.

The distinction may be important in considering employees' rights and employers' liabilities when a paramedical practitioner is working in a general medical practice, clinic or health centre. It may be, according to the particular arrangements which are made, that a practitioner remains an employee of the health authority with which there exists a contract of service. More usually, however, there will be a contract of employment (contract of service) directly between the practitioner and the practice principals or managers of the institution in question.

For the purpose of the following sections the term 'employee' has a common meaning. It should be added, however, that while the law relating to the vicarious liability of an employer for injuries caused by an employee to a third party applies generally to activities within the National Health Service, certain employee rights discussed in the first section are not expressed by relevant employment legislation to be legally binding on health authority employers. Such is the case with written particulars of employment and rights on redundancy. As will be noted, however, health service conditions follow and in places improve on the minimum conditions required by generally applicable employment legislation.

THE EMPLOYMENT CONTRACT

An enforceable contract requires the existence of an agreement supported by what the law calls 'consideration'. Consideration is in effect the price of a bargain. So a promise to pay wages is 'bought' by work done or, more usually, by a promise to work. The law's requirement that an enforceable contract be supported by consideration excludes voluntary workers from the term 'employee' even though they may be doing valuable work in connection with, say, a health authority, hospital or practice.

Written particulars of employment

Perhaps surprisingly, most contracts of employment are not legally required to be in writing. The basic rule in the law of contract generally is that an agreement supported by consideration is enforceable. Naturally, however, the great majority if not all employment relationships which paramedical professionals are likely to encounter will be put in writing.

While the contract itself need not be in writing, the Employment Protection (Consolidation) Act 1978 (s.1) requires an employer to provide an employee with a written statement which identifies the parties to the agreement and specifies the date at which the employment began. The written particulars must also state whether employment with a previous employer counts as part of the employee's 'continuous employment' with the present employer. This notion of continuous employment is important when it comes to considering whether or not a particular employee qualifies for one or more of a variety of rights in job protection, such as the right not to be unfairly dismissed.

Written particulars of employment must, if they are to form part of the employment agreement, be given by an employer to an employee in respect of the following matters: rates or scales of pay; intervals at which the employee is paid (weekly, monthly, etc); hours of work; holiday entitlement; incapacity for work due to sickness or injury, and any provisions for sick pay; pensions and pension schemes; the length of notice required of the employee; and the title of the job which the employee is employed to do.

In addition the Employment Protection (Consolidation) Act requires the statement of written particulars to include a note which specifies any disciplinary rules applicable to the employee, or referring to a document which is reasonably accessible to the employee and which specifies such rules. The statement must also specify or describe a person to whom the employee can go if dissatisfied with a disciplinary decision, or to whom the employee can go to seek redress for a grievance relating to his employment. Any further steps consequent on going to such a person must also be explained in the statement or in a readily accessible document which explains them.

The statement of written particulars must be given to the employee no later than 13 weeks after his period of employment began. It must represent the terms of his employment as at a specified date not more than one week before the statement is given. This means that casual employees do not benefit from the provision in respect of written particulars.

It may occasionally happen that there is a conflict or discrepancy between the written statement and the true terms of employment. Although the statement does not itself constitute the contract of employment, either party to the employment relationship may find it difficult in legal proceedings to deny that the terms contained in the written statement are those under which the employee was in fact taken on in the first place. Both employers and employees should therefore be careful to have an accurate statement of particulars. This is because the actual conduct of either of them in appearing to accept a change from the terms originally agreed may serve to prevent a later reliance on those terms in legal proceedings. If, for instance, the original agreement contained a term which required an employer to give three months' notice, and the written statement in fact says that only one month shall be required, an employee who knows or has reason to know of the discrepancy may be precluded from insisting on the three months' notice as originally agreed.

The requirements of the 1978 Act in respect of written particulars of employment do not apply to the National Health Service and therefore to health authorities and their employees. Nevertheless the normal legal requirements are in practice followed by health authority employers.

Employment provisions affecting paramedical staff

As noted in Chapter 2 in respect of a limited protection of title thereby given, certain regulations made under National Health Service legislation specifically affect the employment of paramedical practitioners in the service. No such restriction is placed by law on employment of paramedical practitioners in hospitals and clinics operating in the independent health care sector, in general medical practices, or in centres outside the control of NHS authorities.

The National Health Service (Professions Supplementary to Medicine) Regulations 1974[1] stipulate that no 'officer' (that is, staff member) shall be employed by a health authority in the capacity of a chiropodist, dietitian, medical laboratory technician, occupational therapist, orthoptist, physiotherapist, radiographer or remedial gymnast unless that person is registered with the appropriate board.

It will be recalled that speech therapists were included until a late stage in arrangements prior to the establishment of the Council for Professions Supplementary to Medicine and its constituent boards, but then withdrew. Special regulations nevertheless apply to the employment of speech therapists in the National Health Service. The National Health Service (Speech Therapists) Regulations 1974[2] provide that no person shall be employed by a health authority in the capacity of a speech therapist unless certain conditions are satisfied. Such a person must either hold a certificate issued by the College of Speech Therapists certifying that he has attended a course of training, and passed an examination, approved by the Secretary of State; or hold such a certificate certifying that the College is satisfied that he has, in a country or territory outside the United Kingdom, attended a course of training and passed an examination recognised by the College and approved by the Secretary of State; or must be included in a list, kept by the Secretary of State, of persons not thus qualified but who have nevertheless satisfied the Secretary of State that their training and experience are adequate for employment as speech therapists.

The fact that these regulations afford some limited protection of title has been noted. What is now to be considered in the context of employment law is a different question. That is, what will be the legal consequences if an unregistered paramedical practitioner, or an unsuitably qualified speech therapist, is employed by a health authority? The dismissal of a person whom regulations provide should not have been taken on in the first place is potentially fair, subject to the further considerations relating to fair and unfair dismissal discussed later in this chapter. If the employing authority in fact continued to employ the unregistered or unqualified person following discovery of the mistake, in order for instance to allow the employee to work out the period of notice under the employment agreement, this would of course be a continued breach of the regulations.

No particular penalty is imposed upon a health authority, and certainly not upon a practitioner who has in good faith entered health authority employment, for the employment being in breach of the regulations. A fraudulent obtaining of an offer of health authority employment would of course give the employing authority the right of summary dismissal.

However, if by some mischance an accident or injury befell a patient undergoing treatment by a paramedical practitioner who did not hold the appropriate qualifications, the health authority would find it that much more difficult to defend a negligence action brought jointly against employee and employer, the latter being sought to be held vicariously liable for the patient's injury.

Employment protection

The Employment Protection (Consolidation) Act 1978 provides for a variety of protections in favour of an employee. They constitute minimum standards and may in fact be improved upon in particular employment contracts, or in nationally negotiated conditions.

An employee who is absent from work owing wholly or partly to pregnancy or confinement is entitled to maternity pay for six weeks of such absence. But such entitlement exists only if she is continuously employed by her employer until immediately before the 11th week prior to the expected weeks of confinement. The period of continuous employment leading up to that time must be at least two years. The six weeks' paid leave may be taken any time after the 11th week before the confinement. An employee absent for this reason is entitled to maternity pay at the rate of nine-tenths of a week's pay for each week of absence. From this will be subtracted any maternity allowance payable under social security legislation (ss. 34, 35).

In addition to these rights to maternity leave and maternity pay, the 1978 Act (as amended in certain respects by the Employment Act 1980) provides for a right to return to work after confinement.[3] An employee who has been absent from work owing to pregnancy or confinement is normally entitled to return to work in the same job in which she was originally employed. The terms and conditions of employment following return to work shall be no less favourable than those under which she would have worked had she not been absent. The right to return to work is dependent on the same conditions which govern rights to maternity leave and pay. That is, the employee in question must have been employed until immediately before the 11th week prior to her confinement, and must at that time have been continuously employed for two years.

The Employment Act 1980 imposes limitations on a woman's rights to return to work in two situations. The first is unlikely to affect more than a very few paramedical practitioners, though it should nevertheless be briefly mentioned. That is, if the employee in question works for an employer who, immediately before her time off work, employed no more than five employees, and it is not reasonably practicable for the employer to permit her to return to work or to offer her suitable alternative employment on terms not substantially less favourable than those in the former job, she will not have the right to return to work. Second, in the case of an employer of any size, if it is not reasonably practicable (for reasons other than redundancy) to permit her to return to work, and suitable alternative employment is offered, again on terms which are not substantially less favourable than those in the old job, and the employee either accepts or unreasonably refuses the new terms, the right to return to the former job is lost.

The practical significance of such limitations on the right to return to work is that, if the employer complies with the requirements of the legislation, the employee will have no claim of unfair dismissal. The subject of unfair dismissal in general is discussed later in this chapter.

A further situation involving protection in employment is provided for in the Employment Protection (Consolidation) Act 1978 in respect of dismissal on account of trade union membership or trade union activities. That, too, will be noted below in relation to unfair dismissal in general. But the 1978 Act also naturally provides (s. 23) job protection in respect of actions which might be taken against him short of dismissal. All employees have a statutory right not to have action short of dismissal taken against them for the following purposes: preventing or deterring the employee from being a member of a trade union, or penalising him for being a member; preventing him or deterring him from engaging in activities of an independent trade union at the appropriate time for such participation, or penalising him for doing so; and, in certain circumstances, compelling the employee to become a trade union member.

The employee's complaint in respect of any such action must be brought within three months of the occurrence or last occurrence complained of. The remedy for violation of an employee's rights in employment short of dismissal is, like the great majority of unfair dismissal cases which succeed against an employer, financial compensation. The object of compensation is just that – to compensate. It is not designed to penalise the employer who has taken action short of dismissal against an employee.

Employment protection rights also extend to entitlements to time off work in certain specified circumstances. An employer is under a legal obligation to allow an employee who is an official of an independent trade union recognised by him to have time off for certain trade union duties (s. 27). These duties involve those concerned with industrial relations between employer and employee, and time off work shall also be allowed to enable an employee to undergo training in aspects of industrial relations relevant to carrying out those duties.

Time off work must also be given to an employee who is a member of an independent trade union recognised by the employer for trade union activities including, for instance, attendance by the employee as a union delegate at a conference. An employer or employing authority must also allow time off for the purpose of performing duties as a justice of the peace, a member of a local authority, a member of a statutory tribunal, a member of a regional or district health authority, a member of the governing body of an educational establishment maintained by a local education authority, and a member of a water authority (s. 29).

Entitlement to time off work in respect of trade union duties, trade union activities and the public duties listed above is not dependent upon the employee's having a qualifying period of continuous employment. But there is no such entitlement in the case of employees who are employed under a contract which normally involves employment for less than 16 hours per week. This is clearly a sensible provision, representing as it does a working compromise between the employee's permission for legitimate time off work and the employer's not being without staff for more than a reasonable proportion of their employed time.

An employee who has been given final notice of redundancy is entitled to time off to look for work or to make arrangements for training. This entitlement is dependent on having been continuously employed for two years or more. It is only weeks of employment of 16 or more hours a week which count towards continuous employment, and so many part-time employees are excluded from this right.

Time off must be allowed for ante-natal care. An employee who is pregnant and who has, on the advice of a registered medical practitioner, registered midwife or registered health visitor, made an ante-natal appointment has a right not to be unreasonably refused time off for the appointment. The employer or employing authority is entitled to ask for a certificate from a doctor, midwife or health visitor that the employee is indeed pregnant, and may also require her to produce some documentary evidence of the appointment such as an appointment card (s. 31A).

It should again be noted that these statutory provisions in respect of employment rights and protection constitute a minimum legal provision and may well be improved upon in individual employments, including employment in the National Health Service.

Disciplinary procedures in employment

The responsibility for drawing up a disciplinary procedure rests with an employer or employing authority. Two points arise here. First, there is no legal requirement as such to draw up such a procedure; but if a procedure exists and is adhered to, each side knows where it stands, and adherence to, or departure from, a disciplinary procedure is the more readily seen as fair or unfair, as the case may be. Second, where a disciplinary procedure is drawn up, joint negotiations between management and staff (the latter frequently represented by trade unions) are apt to create procedures which have a better chance of efficient operation.

Every employer or employing authority is free to draw up a separate disciplinary procedure. In the National Health Service, management and unions representing staff at district level negotiate their own procedures within broad guidelines. In practice, none but very small employers with few staff are likely to be without a disciplinary procedure. Small employers might, for the purpose of employment of paramedical practitioners, include many general medical practices.

The Code of Practice published in 1977 by the Advisory Conciliation and Arbitration Service (ACAS) lists essential features of disciplinary procedures which, though they are not legally obligatory, an employer will be wise to embody in his own disciplinary procedure. Such a procedure should be in writing and should specify to whom it applies. It should provide means whereby action may be quickly taken in matters of discipline. It should indicate the disciplinary actions which may be taken and should specify by whom they may be taken. The Code makes a point of saying that procedures must ensure that immediate superiors do not normally have the power to dismiss without reference to senior management.

Procedures should provide for individuals to be informed of the complaints against them and to be given an opportunity to state their case before decisions are reached. Employees should have the right to be accompanied by a trade union representative or by a fellow employee of their choice. Except in cases of gross misconduct, no employee should be dismissed for a first breach of discipline.

The ACAS Code clearly has rules and principles of natural justice in mind when it adds that procedures should ensure that disciplinary action is not taken until a case has been carefully investigated, and that individuals be given an explanation of any penalty imposed on them. Finally, a right of appeal from a disciplinary decision should be provided, specifying the procedure to be followed in making it.

Termination of the contract of employment

Either employer or employee may lawfully terminate the employment relationship by giving the required notice specified in the contract, subject to an employer's dismissal of an employee being fair. Unfair dismissal is discussed below. Termination of an employment contract without proper notice amounts to wrongful dismissal, and like other forms of breach of contract is dealt with in the ordinary courts of law (unfair dismissal being dealt with in industrial tribunals).

The Employment Protection (Consolidation) Act 1978 lays down (s. 49) certain minimum periods of notice, which may be improved upon in individual instances if the employer and employee so agree. An employee must have been continuously employed for four weeks or more to qualify under the Act. If continuous employment has been less than two years the minimum period of notice is not less than one week. Between 2 and 12 years of continuous employment qualifies an employee for one week's notice for each of those years. And there is a 12-week minimum for those continuously employed for 12 years or more. From employee to employer the minimum notice is one week.

The Act permits such rights to minimum notice to be waived; but even if the right to the period of notice may be waived, the right to pay in lieu of such notice may not (s. 49 (3)). Section 49(5) of the

1978 Act states that the minimum periods of notice do not affect any right of either party to treat the contract as terminable without notice by reason of such conduct of the other party as would have enabled him so to treat it before the passing of the Act. From an employee's point of view this means that an employee can walk out without giving notice if the employer's conduct is such as to entitle the employee to terminate the contract in this way. Conversely, there may be such gross or dangerous misconduct by an employee that the employer is entitled to effect a summary dismissal.

The precise grounds on which a contract of employment can be terminated without notice cannot be predicted in advance. With reference to the summary dismissal of an employee the words of Lord Justice Edmund Davies are instructive as to how times change. In the case of *Wilson v. Racher* (1974) he said:

> Reported decisions provide useful, but only general guides, each case turning on its own facts. Many of the decisions which are customarily cited date from the last century and may be wholly out of accord with current social conditions. What would today be regarded as almost an attitude of Czar-serf, which is to be found in some of the older cases where a dismissed employee failed to recover damages, would, I venture to think, be decided differently today. We have by now come to realise that a contract of service imposes upon the parties a duty of mutual respect.[4]

But while all grounds on which summary dismissal may be justified cannot possibly be specified in advance, obligations such as the duty not to steal the employer's property or deliberately damage it are clearly fundamental. Disobedience to lawful and reasonable instructions might also justify summary dismissal. Single acts of misconduct are less likely as a justification than a persistent pattern, and misconduct at the place of work is more likely to justify summary dismissal than misconduct elsewhere. Justification depends not on the consequences of misconduct but on its nature. Thus an act of misconduct might justify summary dismissal by a health authority even if no patient or other staff member were actually harmed by a potentially very dangerous action.

Unfair dismissal

Unfair dismissal must first be distinguished from wrongful dismissal. The latter is a breach of contract giving rise to an action for damages in the ordinary courts. By contrast an unfair dismissal may be, and usually is, no breach of contract, but nevertheless compensation and certain other legal remedies are available in the following circumstances. Subject to certain exclusions mentioned below, every employee has the legal right not to be unfairly dismissed by his employer. This right is not dependent on contract but is a right to job security and as such an important addition to the job protection outlined earlier in this chapter. The unfairness of a dismissal is not simply a common-sense idea, although it is certainly based on it, for there is a formidable array of tribunal decisions giving the concept a practical meaning in a variety of circumstances. Remedies for unfair dismissal, if successfully proved by an employee, may be financial compensation (97 per cent of successful allegations), reinstatement in the same job, or re-engagement by the same employer.

In the case of *W. Devis and Sons Ltd v. Atkins* (1976) it was said that four questions should be asked when dealing with an allegation by an employee of unfair dismissal. First, was there a dismissal? Second, what was the reason for the dismissal? Third, what events led to the dismissal and why did they lead to it? And, fourth, did the employer act reasonably?

Following section 6 of the Employment Act 1980 a tribunal must take into account various factors, which include the size and administrative resources of the employer's undertaking, in deciding whether an employer acted reasonably.

Certain reasons for dismissal are potentially fair, that is they may be fair or unfair according to circumstances. On the other hand there are some reasons which are automatically unfair. The latter will be examined first before proceeding to those which leave the decision open to the tribunal.

Automatically unfair reasons for dismissal

A female employee is unfairly dismissed if the reason or principal reason for her dismissal is that she is pregnant, or is any other reason connected with her pregnancy. If, however, her pregnancy actually makes her incapable of doing her job properly, her dismissal might be fair. But the employer must act reasonably and must in any event have offered her any suitable alternative work. The Employment Act 1980 imposes restrictions on the right to return to work in these circumstances. No such right exists in the case of small concerns of five employees or less if the employer cannot practicably re-employ or offer suitable alternative employment. And in the case of an employer of any size, there is no such right when return to the job is not reasonably practicable and suitable alternative employment has been offered or unreasonably refused.

It cannot be fair to dismiss an employee for membership of an independent trade union or for participation in union activities, except where there is a 'closed shop'. But that exception to the unfairness of a dismissal is inapplicable if the employee in question objects to trade union membership for reasons of deeply held personal belief.

The Rehabilitation of Offenders Act 1974 provides that a 'spent' conviction shall not be a proper ground for dismissing a person from an office, profession, occupation or employment. This no doubt means that dismissal for such a reason will be automatically unfair. An important exception exists, however, in respect of specified professions, including 'any profession to which the Professions Supplementary to Medicine Act 1960 applies and which is undertaken following registration under that Act'.[5] Oddly, the exception to the unfairness of dismissal on the ground of spent convictions is not expressed to apply to speech therapists, so that the dismissal of a speech therapist for reasons of a spent conviction would be unfair. The discrepancy is no doubt a legislative oversight.

Potentially fair reasons for dismissal

In deciding the question whether the dismissal of an employee was fair or unfair, the employer must show the reason or the principal reason for the dismissal, and must show that the reason was one of the following. Potentially fair reasons include those relating to the capability or qualifications of the employee and to the conduct of the employee. It may be fair to dismiss an employee because of redundancy or because the employee could not continue to work in the position which he held without contravention (either on his part or on that of his employer) of a duty or restriction imposed by or under an enactment. These reasons do not exhaust the possibilities, for it may be fair to dismiss an employee for 'some other substantial reason of a kind such as to justify the dismissal of an employee holding the position which that employee held' (s. 57(1)(b)).

Capability to do the job is assessed by reference to skill, aptitude, health and other physical and mental qualities. In the case of an employee who is absent from work for long periods due to ill health, the employer should consider how long it is reasonable to wait for the employee's return to work. But if dismissal due to incapacity is under consideration the employee should fairly be given an opportunity to state his case, and an independent medical opinion might be sought.

In the case of incompetence to do the job, relevant questions affecting the fairness of dismissal will include whether adequate training and supervision have been given, and whether the employee has been warned about unsatisfactory work.

Misconduct by an employee is commonly a fair reason for dismissal when disciplinary rules relating to the employment have been broken.. The incident must be properly investigated, and in the case of relatively minor offences it must be asked whether a warning ought to have been given as distinct from the final sanction of dismissal. Being late for work would normally require a warning or warnings before dismissal for repeated lateness would be warranted. But theft of or damage to an employer's property and equipment would warrant instant dismissal without warning.

Redundancy may be a fair reason for dismissal, but a failure by the employer to consult the employee or his trade union before selection for redundancy, failure to give reasons, and failure to offer alternative employment may make the dismissal for redundancy unfair. There are two circumstances in which redundancy will always be unfair. First, if the reason for dismissal on account of redundancy is an inadmissible reason, for instance for trade union membership or activities. Second, if the employee is made redundant in breach of a customary arrangement for redundancies in the organisation or undertaking in which the employee works.

It was noted above (p. 33) that regulations impose restrictions on the employment of certain paramedical practitioners in the National Health Service. If, following the appointment by a health authority of an unregistered practitioner in a profession supplementary to medicine in good faith it is subsequently discovered that the appointment was and is in breach of the regulations, dismissal would be potentially fair. But dismissal for this reason would, it appears, not be necessarily fair in all circumstances, and all the facts of a particular case would need to be taken into consideration. It might, for instance, be possible for the employing authority to offer suitable alternative employment, at least until such time as the practitioner in question could obtain registration or otherwise become qualified for employment.

Once the employer has shown that the reason for dismissal was a potentially fair reason, the question of whether or not the particular dismissal was in fact fair is a question for the industrial tribunal, which must decide the question in accordance with equity and the substantial merits of the case. It is not for the employer to prove to the tribunal that his action in dismissing the employee was reasonable.[6]

The Employment Act 1980 provides that, when considering the fairness or unfairness of a dismissal, an industrial tribunal shall take into account the size and administrative resources of the employer's undertaking. For instance, a small undertaking going through difficult times would find it easier to demonstrate the fairness of a dismissal by reason of redundancy than a larger organisation which might be more likely to find suitable alternative employment for the employee in prospect of being made redundant.

Exclusion from protection against unfair dismissal

To be eligible for legal protection against unfair dismissal an employee must have been continuously employed for a period of one year at the date when the employment was terminated. There is no protection against unfair dismissal in the case of employees who have reached normal retiring age before or on the date of termination of the employment. Nor do the unfair dismissal rules apply to those who are employed by their husbands or their wives. No minimum period applies in case of automatically unfair reasons.

Redundancy

It has been noted that redundancy will in certain circumstances be automatically unfair. A general requirement for eligibility for redundancy payment is that the employee shall not have unreasonably refused an offer by the employer of suitable alternative employment, such re-engagement to commence no later than four weeks after the dismissal. Questions as to the suitability of alternative employment and as to the reasonableness or otherwise of refusal are separate, but are in practice often dealt with at one and the same time by tribunals.

Employees dismissed on account of misconduct are not entitled to redundancy payment, since entitlement depends on the dismissal being wholly or mainly attributable to redundancy.

The Employment Protection (Consolidation) Act 1978 which governs eligibility and compensation in respect of redundancy does not apply to the National Health Service. Schemes for redundancy are devised as appropriate.

Unfair discrimination

The Sex Discrimination Act 1975 and the Race Relations Act 1976 make it unlawful for an employer to discriminate on grounds of sex, race or marital status against applicants in selection arrangements and job offers. It is also unlawful to discriminate on those grounds against those who are already employed in respect of access to promotion, training and any other benefits, facilities or services.

FREEDOM OF MOVEMENT WITHIN THE EEC

Paramedical practitioners wishing to practise in another member state of the European Economic Community must ensure that they either possess or acquire the requisite qualifications for practice in the relevant country. Their ambitions will, however, be generally assisted by the anti-discrimination law requiring freedom of movement for workers within the Community. For present purposes the most important aspects of Regulation 1612/68 of the EEC which contains this law are its effects on eligibility for employment and on equality in employment.

Article 3 of this Regulation renders inapplicable any national provision by way either of legal regulation or of administrative action or practice, which explicitly or implicitly limits the rights of foreign nationals to take up and pursue employment. It renders equally inapplicable any such law or administrative practice which subjects recruitment or employment to conditions not applicable in respect of nationals of the member state in question.

Article 7 of the Regulation states that a worker who is a national of a member state may not, in the territory of another member state, be treated differently from national workers because of his nationality in respect of any conditions of employment and work, and in particular pay and dismissal rights and, in the event of unemployment, reinstatement or re-employment rights. Article 7 also requires workers from other member states to have the same access as nationals of the state in question to vocational schools and retraining centres.

The anti-discriminatory Article 3 admits of an exception in the case of special conditions relating to the linguistic knowledge required by reason of the nature of the post to be filled. Language requirements which formerly had to be satisfied by those seeking UK registration as doctors, dentists or nurses were removed. This followed the expression of opinion by the European Commission that these requirements would not always necessarily fall within the exception to Article 3. Health circular HC(81)7 now requires health authority employers to satisfy themselves as to the linguistic ability of applicants for medical, dental and nursing posts in the NHS which safe and reliable communication necessitates.

None of the eight boards for the professions supplementary to medicine makes a linguistic facility a condition of registration, though those boards which are prepared to recognise qualifications gained in non-English-speaking countries will wish to satisfy themselves of the linguistic facility of an applicant for registration. In respect of subsequent practice, circular HC(81)7 states plainly that patients may be endangered and services disrupted if a key member of staff does not speak and understand English properly.

Regulation 1612/68, providing for the inapplicability in the legal regulation and administrative practices of member states of discrimination on grounds of nationality, stops short of making any provision for reciprocal recognition of education and training standards required for qualification and of diplomas and certificates required for professional practice. This latter function belongs to Directives, which are binding as to the end result to be achieved but which leave it to authorities in member states to decide the particular means to achieve that end.

Directives are now in force in respect of the medical and nursing professions but none yet exists for any of the paramedical professions. Particular progress is being made, however, by the physiotherapists. The Standing Liaison Committee of Physiotherapists in the EEC has been meeting for some years. That Committee initiated discussion with the Commission, and suggestions for draft directives affecting training and qualifications have been placed by that Committee before the section of the Commission concerned with the free movement of labour.

VICARIOUS LIABILITY

A further and quite separate incident of the employer-employee relationship from those discussed in the first section of this chapter is the liability of an employer or employing authority for injuries wrongfully caused by employees to third parties, including patients. For the purposes of vicarious liability, reference should again be made to the introduction to this chapter (p. 52) on the distinction between an employee and an independent contractor. It is a contract of service, and not a contract for services, which causes legal liability for third party injuries to fall also upon the shoulders of an employer.

One point must be made clear at once. That is, that the vicarious liability of an employer for the wrongs of his employee is an additional liability to that of the employee himself. The fact that vicarious liability operates in a particular case to hold an employer also liable to compensate the person wrongfully injured does not remove the liability from the shoulders of the employee who actually committed the wrong and caused the injury.

A major underlying objective of the principle of vicarious liability of employers is that of adding a further and usually more substantial opportunity for the injured plaintiff to recover damages in respect of his injuries. Employers are, in the normal run of things, that much more likely to be insured against accidents occurring in the course of their undertaking or at least to be able to pay the plaintiff even if such insurance is not held. In the case of health authorities as employers, damages in respect of third party (including patient) injuries are paid directly out of health authority funds. The National Health Service is for this reason said to be 'self-insuring'.

The course of employment

In order for an employer or employing authority to be vicariously liable for the wrongful act of an employee it must be shown that the latter was acting within the course or scope of his employment. By far the most common form of an employee's wrongdoing is unlawful carelessness, usually the tort of negligence itself (see Chapter 7).

There are cases, however, in which an employer has been liable for the wilful misdeeds and even theft and fraud of an employee.

It might at the outset be asked how a careless act, still more a fraudulent or deliberately criminal act, can possibly be within the scope of employment. The answer is that the law relating to vicarious liability looks at the relationship between employer and employee as a whole and not just at what the employer has stipulated shall be done and what shall not be done by the employee. The apparently remarkable result therefore follows that a fraudulent or even criminal employee could be acting for the purposes of vicarious liability within the scope of his employment, even though as a matter of the employment relationship itself the wrongdoing employee would be liable to summary dismissal.

Detours on journeys

A paramedical practitioner engaged on a domiciliary visit to a patient or client may ask what is the position if a detour is taken from an authorised or expected route to pay a visit to a friend, to take a meal, or for some similar reason. Taking a detour from an unauthorised journey may or may not make a wrongfully caused injury to a third party fall outside the course of employment. The answer may well depend on the particular way in which the question is asked.

On the one hand, it might be asked: was the employee still doing his or her job when taking the detour? On the other hand, a different answer might be given even in the same situation if the question were phrased: had the employee departed altogether from the employer's business or from the job to be done? Put in this second way, detours and departures would be the less likely to fall outside the course of employment. Each case will depend ultimately on its own particular facts, but it appears that legitimate meal breaks, tea breaks and such other comforts will not take the occasion outside the course of employment, and the employer or employing authority would still be vicariously liable if an employee carelessly injured a third party while so engaged. Vicarious liability would be even more likely to apply to an injury caused to a third party when the detour was taken to see another patient in whom the employer or authority had some interest.

Contravention of instructions

The decision in *Rose v. Plenty* (1976) is one of a great many in which employers have been held legally liable to pay damages to injured third parties even when the employee was at the time of the injury contravening an express instruction not to do the very act which caused the damage. This may seem a remarkable result, but a moment's reflection is sufficient to show that an employer could not be permitted to escape the consequences of vicarious liability simply by including a provision in the contract of employment prohibiting the employee from wrongfully injuring a third party. If the courts were to allow such a contract term to exclude an employer's liability, there would be nothing left of vicarious liability.

The position is, therefore, that a contravention of an express instruction may or may not take the employee's act out of the ambit of the employer's vicarious liability. If the act is one which, as in *Rose v. Plenty*, the courts construe as a prohibited way of getting the job done, the employer will still be liable. But if the contravention of instructions has the effect of taking the employee altogether outside the job he is employed to do, as in the case of the unauthorised lift to a stranger in *Twine v. Bean's Express Ltd.* (1946), the employer will not be held to be vicariously responsible for any resulting injuries. The individual employee will, of course, remain personally liable in both cases.

Liability of hospitals and health authorities

In recent years the courts have experienced no difficulty in imposing liability upon a health authority or hospital for injury by any staff, including medical and paramedical staff, to third parties including especially patients. But this has not always been the case. The courts in cases decided some decades ago drew a distinction between the contracts of service of those such as the nursing and other full-time staff, and the contracts for services held by others including medical staff who came from outside to treat patients in the hospital.

The case of *Hillyer v. Governors of St. Bartholomew's Hospital* (1909) arose from a burn injury to a patient caused by a hot water container in the operating theatre. The defendants were held not liable for the injury because their legal liability stopped short at the point of taking reasonable care to assure themselves of the competence of professional staff whom they appointed. Even nurses were regarded as employees of the hospital only for the purposes of their administrative and patient duties, and were not so regarded when assisting a surgeon (who was not an employee but an independent contractor) in an operation.

But in 1942 the law underwent a considerable change in the direction of its present form in a case which in fact involved a radiographer as a co-defendant with the hospital authority. In *Gold v. Essex County Council* (1942) a five-year-old girl was taken by her mother to the hospital maintained by the defendant authority for the treatment of warts on her face. The treatment ordered consisted of 1000–2000 units of Grenz rays and was given by a qualified and competent radiographer who was employed by the authority under a contract of service. The treatment was negligently administered on one occasion, the unaffected parts of her face being covered only with a piece of lint, and the girl's face was permanently disfigured. The trial judge had found in favour of the defendant authority on the basis of the ruling in *Hillyer*'s case, above. But the Court of Appeal reversed his decision and held the authority vicariously liable, drawing a distinction between a contract of service (under which the radiographer was employed) and a contract for services.

A problem still remained, however, in so far as an employee of the defendant hospital or authority would cause the principle of vicarious liability to operate if he did an injurious act on his own account; but the employer would not be vicariously liable to the injured plaintiff if the employee (for instance the radiographer in *Gold*'s case) acted under the instruction of a consultant who was not so employed but who was, rather, an independent contractor to the hospital or health authority.

Gold v. Essex County Council was, it will be noted, decided before the inception of the National Health Service in 1948 as a result of the National Health Service Act 1946. After that date it became much easier to impose liability on hospitals and authorities without the necessity of recourse to fine distinctions between contracts of service and contracts for services. The duty was imposed on the Minister of Health (now upon the Secretary of State for Health and Social Services under sections 1 and 3 of the National Health Service Act 1977) to provide health care, nursing and medical services. It thus became possible to impose liability on a hospital irrespective of whether the person responsible for the patient's injury was an employee or an independent contractor.

In *Cassidy v. Minister of Health* (1951) an operation on the plaintiff's hand went badly wrong, and there had clearly been a want of care on someone's part, though it was not clear precisely on whose. The patient could not attribute negligence to any particular individual, whether employee of the hospital or contractor. Nevertheless Lord Denning (who had been counsel for the successful plaintiff in Gold's case) said:

> . . . when hospital authorities undertake to treat a patient, and themselves select and appoint and employ the professional men and women who are to give treatment, then they are responsible for the negligence of those persons in failing to give proper treatment, no matter whether they are doctors, surgeons, nurses or anyone else.[7]

And in the later case of *Roe v. Minister of Health* (1954), a case which involved paraplegia caused by a contaminated spinal anaesthetic (p. 122), Lord Denning said of the whole of a hospital's staff whether nurses, doctors, anaesthetists or surgeons, and whether full-time or part-time, that the hospital authorities were responsible for all of them. 'The reason', he said, 'is because, even if they are not servants [employees], they are agents of the hospital to give the treatment.' In other words, either the employer–employee relationship or that between principal and agent acting on the principal's behalf is enough to place a primary liability upon the hospital or authority for what went wrong.

Liability and independent contractors

The distinctions drawn at the beginning of this chapter (p. 52) between contracts of service and contracts for services, and the corresponding distinction between employee and independent contractor, are relevant also to the question of liability for the acts of others. In *Gold v. Essex County Council* (1942) the decision hinged on the fact that the negligent radiographer was employed by the authority under a contract of service, that is, he was an employee of the authority. It was simple in that case to impose liability on the authority on that specific basis since no question arose as to the negligence of consultant medical staff.

But in *Cassidy v. Minister of Health* (1951) and *Roe v. Minister of Health* (1954) the possibility arose that consultant staff engaged under contracts for services had been negligent in treating the patients in question. Difficulties were surmounted by fixing primary liability on the hospital or authority.

There are, in addition, certain other circumstances in which liability to injured third parties may fall also upon a person engaging the services of an independent contractor who causes those injuries. The most likely instance of such liability for present purposes is that of an express instruction given to the independent contractor to do some particular act which causes damage or injury. The independent contractor, being in the nature of things a person skilled and experienced in the job for which he has been engaged, may of course refuse to comply with the instruction if he considers it unsafe. (So too, but probably to a lesser extent, can an employee.) But if the independent contractor acts upon the express instruction of the person engaging his specialist services and someone, for instance a patient, is injured in consequence, legal liability will fall upon both. This is not an instance of vicarious liability, but rather of liability falling directly upon the person issuing the instruction. The situation is distinguishable from the normal run of vicarious liability cases in that the latter will impose additional liability on an employer irrespective of any fault on his part.

So, for instance, if a paramedical practitioner acting for a practice or clinic on a consultancy basis and not under a contract of employment were to injure a patient in pursuance of an express instruction from a principal, say a general medical practitioner or proprietor of a private nursing home, to treat the patient in a certain way, liability would fall upon both to the extent that the act and the instruction were both negligent.

REFERENCES

[1] S.I. 1974 No. 494

[2] S.I. 1974 No. 495

[3] Employment Protection (Consolidation) Act 1978 s. 33, as amended by Employment Act 1980 s. 12; EP(C)A 1978 ss. 45–8

[4] [1974] I.C.R. 428, p. 430

[5] Rehabilitation of Offenders Act 1974 (Exceptions) Order 1975 (S.I. 1975 No. 1023), Schedule 1, Pt I

[6] EP(C)A 1978 s. 57(3), as amended by Employment Act 1980 s. 6

[7] [1951] 2 K.B. 343, p. 362

Chapter Five

COMMON LAW AFFECTING SAFETY

This chapter examines the rules of common law relating to an employer's duty in respect of staff safety. Chapter 6 will examine the statutory provisions relating to an employer's duty and also to systems of regulation and compensation other than those provided by common law.

EMPLOYERS' LEGAL LIABILITY TO STAFF

Any person who is employed by another, whether in the National Health Service, in the independent health care sector or in private practice deserves to have safe working conditions. There is a right, one would say, to be safe while in the workplace, wherever it is (p. 80). This is no mere moral or social right, it is also a legal right which exists at common law. The term 'common law' is used to distinguish legal rules and principles which have developed under its wing from those which are the specific creation of statute or statutory regulations. The common law principle of safety in employment is exemplified in particular cases by the rules and decisions which are the subject of this section.

The legal duties now to be examined are duties which the law casts directly and personally on to the shoulders of an employer. 'Personally' means, here, that the liability of the employer is his own, as distinct from arising vicariously through another employee. It does not, of course, mean that in the case of employing companies and health authorities, the individual managers or officials are liable in their personal capacity. It is simply to say that the employing body or authority is legally liable in its *own* right.

The provision of a safe working system

A term frequently used to describe the compendious duty of an employer in respect of employees' safety is 'safe system of work'. It is this duty which is cast directly on to an employer's shoulders and cannot lawfully be shrugged off or delegated. Such a 'delegation' of responsibility will still be within the system of working for which the employer remains legally responsible. To say the duty cannot lawfully be delegated is only to say that an employer or employing authority cannot escape the consequences of the system of working once it is set up.

The duty of an employer to provide a safe system of work is in fact one single and compendious duty. But within the compendium it is possible to identify in the decided cases on the subject four specific heads of responsibility. These are: the duty to appoint competent and properly qualified staff; the duty to provide and maintain safe equipment; the duty to provide and maintain a safe working place; and, generally, the duty to provide and maintain a safe system of work. These four specific implications of the duty in respect of employee safety are now examined, each with specific reference to decided cases.

It should be remembered once again that judicial decisions arise from disputed cases coming to court. The fact that the cases to be discussed do not specifically involve personalia from the paramedical professions is not, of course, to say that the case-law is any the less relevant to their particular circumstances. On the contrary, though the decided cases spring from their own particular facts and circumstances, the rules and principles which it is possible to derive from the cases are of much more general application. Hypothetical examples of the probable application of the rules from decided cases to conditions in the practice of paramedical professions will be given where appropriate.

Duty to employ competent staff

An employer clearly has a legal responsibility to patients or clients of an institution or a practice to take on staff who are competent to do the job envisaged. It is not only patients and clients, however, who may be in some way endangered or put at risk by an incompetent or insufficiently qualified employee. Colleagues themselves may also in some circumstances be put at risk. This may happen because the incompetent member of staff directly endangers colleagues through his or her own independent actions. The danger may, on the other hand, be due to the fact that the incompetent colleague cannot be relied upon in some process which involves co-operation between staff. Incompetence is apt to be doubly dangerous when both colleagues and patients are both put at risk, say in a physical process in which co-operation between colleagues is part of the process of patient treatment.

Examples of incompetently executed co-operation would include, in the case of physiotherapists and remedial gymnasts and perhaps also occupational therapists, incompetent lifting and exercising of patients or incompetent participation in a team with the patient in a process involving physical movement. An example of an individual act of incompetence which might endanger colleagues could be an instance of a medical laboratory scientific officer who was engaged in the process of combining chemicals in ignorance of the potentially explosive effect of certain chemical combinations. It will be recalled from the previous chapter which discussed rights and duties in employment that incapacity or incompetence is a ground which may justify dismissal of the member of staff concerned, depending on the fairness of the dismissal in all the circumstances of the case. Clearly, an incompetent employee who endangers colleagues by his or her lack of adequate ability will in the nature of things be a candidate for a fair dismissal.

The responsibility owed by an employer or employing body or authority to provide competent staff who are safe and reliable to work with falls distinctly short of amounting to a guarantee of colleague-competence. It is true that the legal duty of an employer in respect of staff safety is a high duty which cannot be delegated to another in his place. It is still a duty involving care, though the duty is a relatively high duty actually to see that care is taken.

Training schools

Training schools will have rules of conduct for people following courses at them. If managers or officials come to know, or ought in all reasonableness to know, of potentially dangerous misbehaviour possibly involving misuse of equipment, an injury resulting from such misdeeds might well cause them to be legally negligent and therefore liable to the injured person. The same result would follow whether the injured person and those in overall charge and legally answerable for the injury were related as employee and employer, or employing authority, in the training school (employer's liability) or whether they were not (ordinary negligence).

The duty to provide safe equipment

An employer or employing authority has a duty at common law to use reasonable care in providing safe plant, equipment and appliances. Decided cases under this heading of legal responsibility are more plentiful than those relevant to the previous heading. Equipment and appliances may cover such a wide variety of occupations that each case tends to be decided according to its own particular circumstances, especially in relation to the nature and purpose of the equipment in question. General rules can, however, be derived from the decided cases, and their applicability to a variety of practices in professional paramedical work can be seen by analogy with the following instances of liability.

The legal duty is not only to provide safe equipment and appliances but also to maintain it in a safe condition. Laboratory equipment is an obvious example of equipment which attracts this responsibility, as is equipment for use by practitioners in the remedial professions. In the case of relatively simple equipment the duties to provide and to check with reasonable care will correspondingly be relatively easy to fulfil. But in the case of more complex, and certainly in the case of more dangerous, equipment and appliances the inspection should be that much more frequent and close. Two further specific examples of an employer's general duty to provide and maintain safe equipment are of interest for present purposes. The first involves an employer's provision of transport for staff; the second involves an employer's reliance on a reputable supplier for equipment and appliances which, when delivered for use, display no obvious defect but which nevertheless turn out to be dangerous.

An example of the first type of case is the decision in *Bradford v. Robinson Rentals Ltd.* (1967). A radio service engineer's job included travelling from call to call in a motor van which was used for both transportation and for carrying the necessary servicing equipment. On one occasion, when his employers knew that weather conditions were likely to be severe, he was instructed to undertake a very long journey to change a colleague's old van. Both that van and his own were unheated. Following unsuccessful objections to the instruction to make the journey in the unheated vans the plaintiff van driver went ahead, and suffered frostbite in the process. The length of the journey and the known or reasonably anticipated weather conditions were certainly decisive facts in the case. The decision went in the van driver's favour, it being established that the employer was negligent in insisting on his journey. This type of case will be seen to be relevant also in the context of outwork and domiciliary visits to patients and clients, discussed below.

The second instance of an employer's liability just mentioned, the case of obtaining equipment and supplies from a reputable supplier, resulted in a statute changing a legal rule which seemed fair enough to employers but potentially most unfair to staff. An employer is, as has been noted, subject to a duty to see that employees are reasonably safe in their working conditions. An employer does not, however, guarantee safety. The common law position was therefore that an employer was not legally answerable for an accident caused by a latent defect in a piece of equipment, provided the defect could not have been discovered through the exercise of reasonable care or examination. The House of Lords so ruled in the case of *Davie v. New Merton Board Mills* (1959).

The particular hardship which this legal rule was apt to produce for injured employees was that the supplier of the equipment in question might be based in another country, or even if based in this country might have gone out of business. In recent times the problem of widespread instances of liquidation of manufacturers and suppliers might have aggravated such hardships for employees.

By an Act of Parliament passed in 1969, a full decade after the Law Lords' decision exonerating employers who relied on reputable sources for apparently reliable equipment, the legal position was restored to a more protective situation for staff injured by the equipment. The Employers' Liability (Defective Equipment) Act 1969 established the following principle: an employee, injured in the course of employment due to a defect in equipment provided by the employer, can sue the employer himself (or the authority, or company, as the case may be).

The Act provides that if the defect is due to the fault of a third party, whether identified or not (for instance, one or more foreign manufacturers or a manufacturer in this country who has gone out of business), the employee's injury is deemed to be also due to the negligence of the employer. Employees do not, therefore, have to go to the trouble of identifying a manufacturer and proving him at fault.

A final point of some importance in a variety of practical situations in which members of certain professions supplementary to medicine might find themselves relates to the use of cleaning materials and other substances normally incidental to practice. Some cases of injury (in the sense of physical harm including dermatological conditions) may give rise to problems considered below under the more general heading of 'safe system of work'. Contracting a disease or a skin condition from a patient or client would be an example.

Maintaining a safe place of work

The duty of an employer in respect of employee safety being in effect but one duty, many of the incidents of the duty to maintain a safe place of work will normally be subsumed under the more general heading of providing a 'safe system'. But, again, two particular instances of possible legal liability fall to be discussed specifically under this present heading. Both concern the extent and ambit of the duty to maintain a safe working place.

The case of *Davidson v. Handley Page Ltd.* (1945) concerned the liquid known as 'suds' which were used for cleaning lathes. The employee in question was employed in one of the company's workshops in which there was a row of vats containing the suds. This liquid was frequently spilled by lathe operators while they were carrying it from the vats to the lathes and the floor was very slippery as a result. Workers were employed to clean the floor and to put sawdust on it from time to time.

Above the rows of vats was a water tap. Access to the tap and the vats was gained by standing on a duck-board, or loose wooden board. The plaintiff went to the tap to wash a teacup for her own use and was injured when she slipped on the duckboard. At the time of the accident suds had been splashed on it and no sawdust had been put down. The judge ruled against her in an action for damages brought by her against the employers. The Court of Appeal reversed the judge's decision, however, and in so doing established an important principle. This is, that the obligation of an employer to provide safe appliances and a safe place of work extends to cover all acts which are normally and reasonably incidental to the daily work. The employer's case was therefore covered by this principle in the present instance and she was awarded damages against her employers.

A tea-break is therefore normally incidental to a day's work. It may also be assumed that normal and reasonable breaks and recreational aspects of a working day, for instance brief exercise, are expected to fall within normal activities. If injury occurs in, or in connection with, such intervals or reasonable recreation, a legal duty of care in the employer or employing authority may accordingly be expected to exist.

Domiciliary visits

The second point of particular importance under the present head of legal liability concerns a much more literal sense of the ambit of working conditions for which an employer may be legally responsible. The question may arise as to what liability an employer or employing authority has in relation to work done away from base, so to speak. Many practitioners in the professions supplementary to medicine will have to make domiciliary visits to their patients and clients. The liability of the occupier of the premises in which treatment or consultation takes place is discussed in Chapter 8. Our present concern is to consider whether, quite separately from any question of liability on the part of the occupier, the employers may themselves be legally liable for the conditions in which their employed practitioners are instructed to work.

The case of transportation on practice business has already been discussed. The decision in *Bradford v. Robinson Rentals Ltd.* (p. 77) shows that transportation which is supplied by an employer, which is necessary to the job to be done, and which is defective may lead to legal liability to an injured employee. The unheated van in that case was insufficient protection against the fiercely bad winter of 1963, and the driver suffered frostbite. This injury was unusual for this country, but not so unusual as to be impossible to envisage.

As regards the safety of the place of destination itself, it used to be thought that an employer, having no control over the other premises in question, could accordingly be subject to no legal duty to employees in respect of those premises. The opposite view is now, however, accepted as representing the law. Any difference between the maintaining of safe working premises in the actual occupation of the employer, and being reasonably careful in respect of premises in the occupation of others but within which his employees are expected or instructed to work, relates only to the kind of precautions to be taken and not to the existence of the duty itself.

The principal source of legal guidance on circumstances which could include outwork and domiciliary visits by practitioners, more especially perhaps in the remedial professions but not exclusively, is the case of *Wilson v. Tyneside Window Cleaning Co.* (1958). In the case itself it was held that a 56-year-old window cleaner with a life-long experience in the trade could not recover damages from his employers. He had been cleaning a window in a brewery from the outside. A handle on which he had been supporting himself gave way, and he fell and was injured. He had often cleaned the window before and knew that the woodwork was unsound. Experience had also taught him that it was unsafe to trust handles.

In an action for negligence against his employers he claimed that they should have inspected the premises on which he was called upon to work, and that they should have issued oral and written warnings against the dangers of window cleaning in general, and those connected with unsafe handles in particular. The court decided that in the case of a workman so experienced, and of a danger which was so obvious, the issue or repetition of warnings would in fact have been more likely to do harm than good.

The case is important not so much for its result, which is unsurprising, but rather for the guidance stated by two of the Lords Justices of Appeal who decided the case in the Court of Appeal. Speaking of an employer's legal duty to employees, Lord Justice Parker (later Lord Chief Justice) said:

> That general duty applies in the circumstances of every case; but the governing words 'reasonable care' limit the extent of the duty in the circumstances of each case. Accordingly, the duty is there whether the premises on which the workman is employed are in the occupation of the master [employer] or of a third party . . . but what reasonable care demands in each case will no doubt vary.

More specifically, Lord Justice Pearce said:

> Whether the servant [employee] is working on the premises of the master or those of a stranger, that duty is still, as it seems to me, the same; but as a matter of common sense its performance and discharge will probably be vastly different in the two cases. The master's own premises are under his control; if they are dangerously in need of repair he can and must rectify the fault at once if he is to escape the censure of negligence. But if a master sends his plumber to mend a leak in a respectable private house, no one could hold him negligent for not visiting the house himself to see if the carpet in the hall creates a trap.[1]

Having thus given two entirely different examples, in which the respective answers would clearly differ, Lord Justice Pearce continued to state the general rule of law:

> Between these extremes are countless possible examples in which the court may have to decide the question of fact: Did the master take reasonable care so to carry out his operations as not to subject those employed by him to unnecessary risk? Precautions dictated by reasonable care when the servant works on the master's premises may be wholly prevented or greatly circumscribed by the fact that the place of work is under the control of a stranger. Additional safeguards intended to reinforce the man's knowledge and skill in surmounting difficulties may be reasonable in the former case but impracticable and unreasonable in the latter. So viewed, the question whether the master was in control of the premises ceases to be a question of technicality and becomes merely one of the ingredients, albeit a very important one, in a consideration of the question of fact whether, in all the circumstances, the master took reasonable care.

Within this broad guidance, each case will depend on its own particular circumstances. A vital feature of cases involving domiciliary visits is likely to be the knowledge, or otherwise, of the employer or employing authority of a dangerous condition in premises to be visited. Except in most unusual circumstances an employer is unlikely to be legally liable for a dangerous condition on premises which are visited for the first time on a domiciliary care basis. In the words just quoted, it would be quite unreasonable to place a burden on an employer so great that he or an agent on his behalf had first to check all outside premises as though they were his own.

On the other hand the first or a subsequent visit to a patient's home might reveal a danger to the practitioner in question. If that danger were reported back, and if nothing were to be done about it, and injury were to befall the practitioner in consequence, legal liability might well fall on the employer's shoulders. Such dangers might arise from the conditions of the premises, such as a faulty staircase or a door which was coming off its hinges and unsafe; or it might even arise from the behaviour of the occupier of the premises. Cases do arise from time to time of assaults on health service staff, general medical practitioners, and practitioners engaged in treating or supervising patients on a domiciliary basis.

In so far as working conditions in the National Health Service are concerned a DHSS circular issued in 1976 is useful. The contents of the circular are examined after the conclusion of the present examination of the legal liability of an employer. It should, however, be remembered that if an employer knew or ought to have known about a vicious or otherwise dangerously unpredictable tendency in a patient to be visited at his or her home, the duty of the employer to provide a safe working place might in some cases be broken if injury resulted to the employee practitioner. Mental disorder can produce violent propensities, although a great many mentally disordered people are remarkably predictable.

A safe system of work

An employer's duties in respect of the appointment of qualified and competent staff, safe and reliable equipment, and safe place and surroundings of work whether these be the employer's own or those in the occupation of some other person, have been elaborated in detail. Most further comment would therefore be redundant. There are, however, two concluding comments to make in respect of the very *system* in which each of the elements already examined plays its part.

For one thing, a working system based on efficient and clear communications is essential where most forms of teamwork and co-operative practice are involved. For another, if safety precautions, such as protective equipment, are a normal or necessary adjunct of a particular job, it is up to employers to take adequate steps to bring the precautions to the attention of the staff involved. Language problems will again be difficulties to be guarded against when it comes to making safety precautions clear to staff. But an employer does not owe such a high duty in this respect that he has to stand over employees to ensure that they observe the precautions. It is sufficient if they are brought reasonably to the attention of the employee.

Able-bodied staff are normally taken to consent to risks ordinarily incidental to the work in which they are employed. Provided, of course, the danger or injury does not result from someone else's negligence. In *Michie v. Shenley and Napsbury General Hospital Management Committee* (1952) a male nurse employed at the hospital brought an action for damages against the health authority for damages in respect of injuries received from an epileptic patient. The injuries had been caused by a physical attack on the nurse. He failed in his action. The judge held that a mental nurse chose his occupation knowing that it was subject to certain hazards. One such hazard was, he ruled, the unpredictable conduct of mental patients, epileptics or others. He said that any person making the care of mental patients his life work must have some expectation of assault and violence. It so happened that on the night on which the attack took place the nurse had had the clearest warning from the patient's behaviour that there was a likelihood of his becoming violent. It was proved in evidence that there were in fact a number of ways in which the plaintiff nurse could have obtained assistance. He should, the judge ruled, have shown greater care for his own safety by getting help before approaching the patient.

The possible implications of this decision for practitioners in professions supplementary to medicine are interesting. Such people, including especially members of the remedial professions, encounter mentally disordered patients otherwise than in a nursing capacity. Unless these practitioners are engaged full-time in a mental hospital (say, as a resident occupational therapist), it might well be that the decision in such a case as the one discussed above would go the other way. On the other hand, for instance, an occupational therapist engaged full-time in work with mentally disordered patients might be held to have become familiar with unpredictable behaviour. Unusual behaviour, if frequently repeated, becomes predictable. Each case will again depend upon its own particular circumstances.

Finally, what of injury at work caused not by an external force such as the one just discussed, but by an internal weakness or condition exacerbated by the particular work involved in the job. Again, examples of physical stress and other movements necessary in the case of the remedial professions come to mind. The following case is instructive in some circumstances of work injury.

In *Parkes v. Smethwick Corporation* (1957) the plaintiff was employed as an ambulance driver by the defendant employers. Before he started his job with them he had suffered a hernia, but he had not told them about it. Ambulance drivers had from time to time complained to their employers that their work was heavy and awkward. It had been suggested that retractable stretcher gear be fitted to the ambulances but this had not been done. This driver suffered a hernia when lifting a patient into an ambulance, and he sued his employers in respect of the injury.

It was held by the court that the defendant employers were under no legal duty to examine the ambulance driver to see if he was fit for that work, or to fit all their ambulances with retractable gear. If the employers knew or ought reasonably to have known about the previous hernia the result could well have been different.

VIOLENT PATIENTS: THE HEALTH CIRCULAR

This chapter has examined an employer's common law safety duties in relation to the facts of particular cases. A useful addition of broader relevance is the guidance given in health circular HC(76) 11. Violence may arise in connection with the treatment and rehabilitation of mentally disordered persons, but experience of violence by health care staff is by no means limited to that context.

Acts of violence from patients have been encountered particularly in the cases of accident and emergency departments and the treatment of mental patients. Arrangements for adequate supervision and prediction of potentially violent patients are strongly recommended. Cases of alcoholism and drug dependence in patients should be especially noted and provided against. An employing authority should arrange for readily accessible and effective means of quickly summoning assistance in the event of a violent incident. 'The number of staff on duty in a department, ward or group of closely linked wards should at all times be enough to meet this need', says the circular. Training and the ensuring of staff awareness of the possible risks incidental to their employment in the presence of potentially violent patients are recommended.

Every hospital should have an adequate system for recording and reporting any incident involving violence by a patient. This step should be taken whether or not the violent incident in question has resulted in personal injury to any person or in damage to property. 'All incidents of violence should be followed by discussion between the doctors and the other members of the team responsible for the patient's treatment, to determine the causes and whether any change in approach is required.'

Personal injury to an employee may qualify that person for social security benefits in respect of the injury. And any injured person, whether or not injured during employment, may qualify under the Criminal Injuries Compensation scheme. These statutory arrangements are examined in the following chapter.

HAZARDS IN HEALTH CARE

Given the enormous variety and mass of equipment used in health care services it is not to be wondered that defects are sometimes discovered. Some defective equipment may, however, put staff at risk, in addition to creating possible danger to patients. The DHSS accordingly operates a hazard notification system which was revised and streamlined in 1981.[2]

Accidents and defects concerning medicinal products, equipment and other supplies used in the National Health Service may be reported to the DHSS by either the health authority involved or by the manufacturer or supplier. Notification made as early as possible warns health authorities of the actual or potential risks to patients, staff, visitors and the general public, as the case may be. Advice is simultaneously given on the appropriate steps to be taken to remove or minimise those risks.

The hazard notification system comprises three 'levels' of information and is intended to distinguish between risks considered to be extremely hazardous, demanding immediate action and having a priority classification; risks which are hazardous and require urgent remedial action; and the giving of more general advice on hazard prevention. Items included in the third category relating more generally to concern with safety include advice on safety standards as well as information from the Health and Safety Executive. The Health and Safety at Work Act 1974 is considered in the following chapter.

It may, however, be noted in the context of an examination of the common law duty to provide safe equipment and supplies that hazard notices may affect legal liability. If a health authority for some reason omitted to act in reasonable time upon a hazard warning so circulated and injury resulted to an employee, a common law action for damages would probably succeed. The legal duty of care underlying injury liability would have been broken by the failure to act when the employing authority ought reasonably to have done so.

FAULT OF THE EMPLOYEE

Even if an employer is found to be in breach of a legal duty as examined in this chapter, it may be that the employee showed some lack of care for his or her own safety. Damages may in that case be reduced on account of the employee's contributory negligence. If, for instance, it is decided that both parties are equally to blame, damages will be half of what would otherwise have been awarded in the absence of the employee's fault.

DISCLAIMER OF LIABILITY

An employer may not, either by a notice displayed at work or by the terms of a contract, disclaim liability for work injury to an employee. Such a term or notice is prohibited by section 2(1) of the Unfair Contract Terms Act 1977, which prohibits the exclusion or restriction of liability in negligence for personal injury or death.

REFERENCES

[1] [1958] 2 Q.B. 110, p. 121
[2] HN(81)21

Chapter Six

STATUTORY LAW AFFECTING SAFETY

EMPLOYERS' LIABILITY INSURANCE

It is appropriate to begin this outline of the impact of statutes and regulations on health, safety and injury law with a comment on a statute directly connected with the rules of liability for work injury examined in the previous chapter.

The Employers' Liability (Compulsory Insurance) Act 1969 places a legal duty upon most employers to maintain a policy of insurance covering work injury liability to employees. Insurance is required to be maintained against liability for bodily injury and disease suffered by employees and arising in or out of their employment. The insurance must cover liability of at least £2m arising out of any one occurrence.

The Act imposes this duty to insure upon any person or body carrying on a trade or business. Independent hospitals and clinics are clearly within the Act, as are general medical practices which employ staff. The Act applies to employers in respect of their injury liability to employees. Rules and judicial decisions examined in Chapter 5 are therefore relevant in first determining whether the employer has in fact incurred any injury liability to the employee in question. The object of the 1969 Act is to insure against the financial consequences of injury claims successfully made against an employer. It is not to insure against injury claims made independently of allegations of legal liability.

A further and independent ground of an employer's liability, namely for injury arising from the breach of a statutory duty, is discussed in the following section of this chapter.

There are certain exceptions mentioned in the Act to the obligation to insure against injury or disease liability. The principal exception for the purposes of this book exists in the case of the National Health Service. The NHS as an employer (of a great many staff, more than one million in all) is not covered by the Act. The health service is said to be 'self-insuring'. This means that the cost of successful liability claims is met out of the annual budget of health authorities. Legal liability in damages is thus catered for in the same way in respect of both employees and patients.

Breach of statutory duty

Legal liability of an employer to compensate an injured employee may result from a failure to maintain a safe system of work. It may also arise from an employee's injury caused by the breach of a duty imposed on an employer by a statute or by regulations. These sources of legal obligation are normally principally concerned with the enforcement of a certain course or standard of conduct. A breach of duty may result in the imposition of a criminal penalty, usually a fine. But where does an injured employee stand? Such a person's principal interest will be in compensation for himself, not in seeing his employer fined.

In some instances a statute or regulations made under it may specifically state that breach of the duty shall, or shall not, be a ground for civil liability in damages to a person injured. Regulations, for instance, made under the Medicines Act 1968 are expressly stated by section 133 of that Act to exclude a civil right of action in any person in the event of breach, unless a particular regulation provides otherwise.

An example of the opposite statutory policy is found in the Sex Discrimination Act 1975. Section 66 of that Act specifically provides for 'civil proceedings in like manner as any other claim in tort for breach of statutory duty'. Furthermore, as will be noted later, regulations made under the Health and Safety at Work Act 1974 are expressed by that Act to give a civil remedy in damages in the event of breach, unless such a civil remedy is specifically excluded by the regulation in question (p. 101).

A very large number of statutory duties, many of them relating to safety and injury at work, existed before the 1974 Act. In a great many, perhaps the majority of cases, no guidance is given in the statutes or regulations in question as to whether proof of breach is intended to be the basis not only of criminal proceedings but also of an action for damages on the part of the person injured.

Over the years, however, the courts have developed certain rules by which to decide whether civil liability should arise out of the breach of a statutory duty.

First, the person seeking redress by way of damages must show that he or she is within the category or class of people for whose benefit the duty is imposed by the particular statute or regulation.

Second, it must be shown that the injury or damage which occurred was of the kind which the statute or regulation desired to prevent. An action in negligence (that is, breach of a duty of care leading to injury or damage) may still succeed if the action based on breach of statutory duty fails.

Third, in addition to proof that the statutory duty was in fact broken, there must be proof that the breach caused the damage. If an employer failed to provide protective clothing or equipment to an employee and was in breach of duty by so doing, the injured employee's claim would fail if it could be shown that the employee would have omitted or even refused to wear it or use it anyway.

The following conclusion may be drawn as to the relationship between a civil action for breach of a statutory duty and an action in negligence independent of any such statutory duty. In some cases negligence may be proved without there having been a civilly actionable breach of the statute or regulation. In other cases an action for damages founded on breach of the statutory duty may fulfil all the requirements noted above, even if common law negligence or a failure to maintain a safe system of work cannot for some reason be proved. Not every breach of a statutory duty will necessarily be negligence.

Criminal Injuries Compensation

Even if an employee is unable to succeed in an action for failure to maintain a safe system of work, or for injury caused by the breach of a statutory duty, recourse may be had to criminal injuries compensation if the injury in question was caused by a criminal offence involving violence. Such injury might be received from a patient, or even (unusually) from a fellow employee or colleague. The Criminal Injuries Compensation Board, established in 1964, is empowered to make *ex gratia* payments to persons injured as a direct result of crimes of violence. Motoring offences are excluded from the Board's powers unless the offence in question involves a deliberate harmful act to the person applying for compensation.

The circumstances of the injury may have been the subject of criminal proceedings. But even if they have not, an application for compensation may still be made if the circumstances of the injury were reported to the police without delay. Applicants must in every case give the Board every reasonable assistance, including the provision of relevant medical reports.

In some circumstances the Board may waive the requirement that the incident shall have been reported to the police without delay. A circular issued to hospital administrators by the Department of Health and Social Security in 1971[1] concerns injuries to staff in mental hospitals. Chiropodists and practitioners in the remedial professions may be concerned with this matter. It is not the Board's practice to reject applications from staff in mental hospitals because the incident has not been reported to the police. The letter says:

> Provided the Board are satisfied that the full circumstances of the injury have been reported to the hospital authorities without delay, the Board will waive the requirement. The Board stress, however, that the manner of reporting must be such as to enable a proper decision to be made by the hospital authority whether or not police intervention is appropriate: a mere note in an accident or occurrence book may not therefore be sufficient.

It may happen that injury caused by a violent criminal offence will indicate the breach by an employer of his common law duty to maintain a safe system of work. For instance, a deliberate and violent physical assault by a joker or a colleague or patient with known (or reasonable knowable) tendencies to violence, may indicate an employer's failure to employ and maintain a competent and reliable staff or a reasonably safe working system (Chapter 5).

Criminal injuries compensation may provide an alternative avenue of redress for an employee who cannot demonstrate in an employer either breach of the common law duty to provide a safe system of work, or the breach of a statutory duty giving grounds for damages in civil proceedings.

STATUTORY SAFETY SYSTEMS

It is now appropriate to examine safety rules and policies enshrined in statutes of special importance. For purposes of this book these statutes are the Factories Act 1961, the Offices, Shops and Railway Premises Act 1963 and, of course, the Health and Safety at Work Act 1974. The two former statutes are of the same type, establishing an elaborate and detailed statutory safety code for the protection of employees (and in some instances of visitors and members of the public). The Health and Safety at Work Act is of a different type, establishing as it does a unified and streamlined statutory framework for the eventual replacement of the majority of safety provisions, in a variety of places, by one enormous and comprehensive code of safety regulations. Even a decade after the 1974 Act, however, it is still necessary to consider the provisions of the other two statutes since most of their provisions are still in force.

The Factories Act 1961

A factory is defined by section 175(1) of this Act as any premises in which or within the close or curtilage or precincts of which persons are employed in manual labour in any process for or incidental to (a) the making of any article or part of any article, or (b) the altering, repairing, ornamental finishing, cleaning or washing or the breaking up or demolition of any article, or (c) the adapting for sale of any article . . . being premises in which the work is carried on by way of trade or for the purposes of gain and to or over which the employer of the persons employed therein has the right of access and control.

Section 175(2) further extends the definition of 'factory' to include: any premises on which the business of sorting any articles is carried on as a preliminary to any work carried on in any factory or incidentally to the purpose of any factory; any premises in which the business of washing or filling bottles or containers or packing articles is carried on incidentally to the purpose of any factory; any laundry carried on as ancillary to another business or incidentally to the purposes of any public institution; any premises in which printing by letterpress, lithography or photogravure, or other similar process, or bookbinding is carried on by way of trade or for purposes of gain or incidentally to another business so carried on; any premises in which mechanical power is used in connection with the making or repair of articles of metal or wood incidentally to any business carried on by way of trade or for the purpose of gain; and any premises in which articles are made or prepared incidentally to the carrying on of building operations or works of engineering construction, not being premises in which such operations or works are being carried on.

All hospital laundries are therefore within the extended definitions of 'factory' for the purposes of the Factories Act's requirements. This is the case in both NHS and independent hospitals.

The elements of 'trade' and 'gain' which recur in the above definitions are no doubt satisfied in the case of enterprises in the independent sector. They would normally be absent in the case of most activities in NHS premises, but section 175(9) of the Factories Act extends the Act to any premises belonging to or in the occupation of the Crown or any public authority. Such premises could otherwise be excluded since the work carried on there is not generally for 'trade or gain'.

The clerk of works department in a hospital building programme could fall within the extended definition; and the tailor's shop in a mental hospital would fall within the definition also. In *Wood v. L.C.C.* (1940) a court decided that a hospital kitchen is not a 'factory' within the meaning of the Act. But in *Bromwich v. National Ear, Nose and Throat Hospital* (1980) it was held that the definition included a hospital workshop used as and when necessary for mechanical and electrical repairs and minor installation work for the hospital. (Incidentally, the case is thus reported, though the name of the hospital in question is in fact the Royal National Throat, Nose and Ear Hospital.)

The practitioners in professions supplementary to medicine who are perhaps most likely to be concerned with the above Factories Act definitions in respect of premises or parts of premises are occupational therapists. Their work might involve one or more of the creative and manufacturing activities specified in the definitions. Such work could, in particular, include 'the making of any article or part of any article' as specified in the principal definition of 'factory' in section 175(1) of the 1961 Act.

Activities falling within the requirements of the Act itself attract obligations relating to cleanliness, temperature, lighting and the drainage of floors. Probably the most important requirement of the Act, in so far as resulting compensation for physical injury falls to be considered, is the requirement relating to the fencing of machinery. As a general rule, section 14 of the 1961 Act requires every dangerous part of any machinery to be securely fenced unless it is in such a position or of such construction as to be safe to every person working or employed in the premises as it would be if securely fenced.

In the same context of activity, an example of safety regulations made under powers given for that purpose by the principal Act is found in the Protection of Eyes Regulations 1974.[2] These regulations provide for the protection of eyes of persons employed in factories and other places to which the 1961 Act applies while any of a list, in Schedule 1 of the Regulations, of 35 activities is being carried on. Among many other activities that list includes: the breaking, carving or drilling by means of a power-driven portable tool or by a hammer, chisel, pick or similar hand-tool, of any one or more of a number of listed substances. These include glass, hard plastics, fired clay and similar materials, and include also bricks, tiles or blocks, excepting wooden blocks.

Where, in any of these instances, there is a reasonably foreseeable risk of injury to the eyes of any person engaged in the work from particles or fragments thrown off, the duties imposed in the main body of the Regulations apply. These include principally the issue to those in such foreseeable danger of suitable eye protection.

It might also happen that persons concerned with the subject matter of this book, though not acting as occupational therapists in conditions to which the above rules might apply, suffer injury on hospital or other premises within the statutory definition.

In these cases, as in the specific cases of risks in occupational therapy mentioned above, recovery of damages by reason of the breach of a statutory duty applicable to a relevant part of the premises would depend upon the precise wording of the particular regulation in question. If, as is likely, no specific answer could be found in the regulations in respect of liability in damages to the injured person, the rules of construction outlined earlier in this chapter would need to be applied. In this way the court would determine whether or not the breach of the statutory duty or regulation in question should give rise to civil liability in damages to the injured person. It may be recalled in this connection that health and safety regulations made under the Health and Safety at Work Act 1974 will give grounds for civil liability unless they expressly provide otherwise.

It may even happen in some cases that the protection of a statutory duty in respect of civil liability for personal injury will not be removed even if the person injured was at the time of the injury in an unauthorised part of premises which nevertheless falls within the definition of relevant premises given by the particular statute or regulation in question.

The Offices, Shops and Railway Premises Act 1963

This somewhat cumbrously worded title serves simply to indicate the variety of premises to which this later statute applies. The Act closely follows the spirit and objectives of the Factories Act 1961. The Act applies to all offices, that is, any building or part of a building which is used for administration, handling money, operating telephones or other clerical work. It is therefore clear that the Act's potential application to the administrative and associated tasks of all paramedical practitioners is considerable.

For instance, offices in hospitals, clinics, health centres and medical practice premises fall within the Act. They may do so even if the rest of the building is not so included. But in order for the particular part of the premises to fall within the 1963 Act, the administrative or clerical work must be the sole or principal purpose of that part. Therefore the area of a ward in which clerical work is done, even necessarily done, by nursing or paramedical staff will not fall within the Act. A medical laboratory would not fall within the Act merely because a certain amount of paperwork was required in connection with the activities carried on there. But a separate office devoted principally to such administrative and clerical work would probably be covered.

The Act also applies to stairs, passage ways, entrance halls and storerooms in the same building and occupied by the same person or body, if they adjoin premises or parts of premises falling within the Act and used for 'office' purposes. Indeed, any part of the premises used in connection with the main purpose is also covered, including lavatories, washrooms and canteens for 'office' workers. A hospital canteen used for medical, paramedical and nursing staff as well as the administrative and clerical staff would be outside the Act's provisions. Its use would not be solely or principally in connection with office activities.

The Act applies to National Health Service hospitals and other premises in so far as its provisions may give rise to an action in tort (a civil action) for breach of duty. Although the Health and Safety Executive may inspect NHS premises, the Act gives no power to prosecute the NHS in the courts in respect of breaches of the Act amounting to criminal offences. Thus, while an NHS hospital cannot be compelled to comply with obligations imposed by the Act in respect of cleanliness, temperature, lighting and so forth, an injury caused by the breach of a statutory obligation, say to provide an adequate handrail on a staircase to an office, would be civilly actionable at the instance of the person injured. Outside the NHS, namely throughout the independent health care sector and in premises, including general practice premises, privately owned, the Act applies both in respect of inspection and of actionable injury resulting from breach of statutory duty.

The Health and Safety at Work Act 1974

The Factories Act 1961 and the Offices, Shops and Railway Premises Act 1963 are both, as their names indicate, concerned with providing safety codes, regulations and practices in respect of premises. By contrast, the Health and Safety at Work Act 1974 has as its principal objective a system of health and safety practices with attention to people. Many people are brought within the statutory system of health and safety protection who fall outside the provisions of the Factories Act and the Offices, Shops and Railway Premises Act on account of the premises in which they work.

Thus, employees in hospitals other than those who were already covered in respect of safety protection because of some particular area therein being a 'factory' or an 'office', are brought within the safety policies of the 1974 Act. Universities, which are not carried on 'for gain' and which are not therefore included in the factories legislation, also fall within the 1974 Act, its attention being not to premises as such but to people employed on them. Medical laboratory scientific officers working in university medical laboratories therefore fall within the ambit of the 1974 Act.

Section 2(1) of the Health and Safety at Work Act imposes a legal duty on every employer to ensure so far as is reasonably practicable the health, safety and welfare at work of his employees. 'Employee' is a person employed under a contract of service, and includes a trainee and an apprentice. This general duty is owed to employees 'at work'. A person may still be 'at work' even if he is not at a particular moment engaged in the particular job he is employed to do. Thus a person may be 'at work' for the purpose of this most general health and safety duty while preparing or clearing away equipment or taking a normal meal break. In most cases, however, travelling to and from work will fall outside the protection owed by an employer under section 2(1).

Section 2(3) of the Act requires an employer to issue a written statement of his general policy with respect to health and safety at work of his employees, and the organisation and arrangements for the time being in force for carrying out that policy, and to bring the statement and any revision of it to the notice of all his employees.

Section 3 marked a new departure in health and safety law. Both employers and self-employed are obliged so to conduct their undertakings as to ensure that those who are not in their employment should not be exposed to risks to their health and safety. So, for example, potentially hazardous equipment and substances used in a variety of paramedical practices and professions supplementary to medicine have to be used and cared for in such a way as to avoid exposing others, including patients or clients, to risk.

Duties of employees in respect of health and safety

While the principal thrust of the 1974 Act is aimed, not unnaturally, at employers, the duties imposed by the Act extend also in some cases to employees. The duty of an employer to maintain a healthy, safe and reliable system may depend very much in certain cases on positive employee participation. And in the negative sense, a health and safety policy might be spoiled or endangered by omissions or wrongdoing on the part of employees.

An employee whose job includes a specific health and safety responsibility, imposed by his employment contract or which he has agreed to take on, must do his reasonable best to fulfil the requirements of that duty. Furthermore, employees in general have a statutory duty to assist their employer in the maintenance and implementation of safety schemes and practices.

The Health and Safety at Work Act provides for a number of means of enforcement, the ultimate of which is a criminal penalty (normally a fine). Before dealing with enforcement provisions as a whole in the following section of this chapter, it is convenient to note briefly at this point the relevance of criminal sanctions to individual employees under the Act.

The general positive duties, some of which have been noted, in respect of participation in and co-operation with health and safety policies and practices, are incumbent on employers and employees alike. While the criminal enforcement of these provisions always remains an ultimate possibility in the case of individual employees, the omission or failure to discharge a general or particular safety duty will have to be an extremely serious matter if prosecution is to be considered.

If criminal prosecution is to occur, a more probable ground in the case of an individual employee is to be found in section 8 of the 1974 Act:

> No person shall intentionally or recklessly interfere with or

misuse anything provided in the interests of health, safety or welfare in pursuance of any of the relevant statutory provisions.

So, for instance, a remedial therapist would only be within the scope of this wrongdoing (which is a criminal offence under section 33 of the Act) if there was a deliberate, possibly perverse, misuse of equipment. Mere omission or negligence will not fall within the definition of conduct which is intentional or reckless. As noted above, however, an extremely serious omission to discharge a duty in respect of health and safety of the participatory or co-operative type mentioned above could lead to prosecution.

Health and safety enforcement powers

The Health and Safety at Work Act contains detailed enforcement powers in respect of the Factories Act and the Offices, Shops and Railway Premises Act. The enforcement powers contained in those statutes are repealed and replaced in regulations made under the 1974 Act. In addition, broad and important new enforcement powers are introduced into health and safety law by the Health and Safety at Work Act itself.

In addition to the ultimate sanction of a criminal penalty, mentioned above in respect of employees but applicable also to employers, powers are given to inspectors acting on behalf of the Health and Safety Executive to discharge a wide variety of functions. Section 20 of the Act confers powers on inspectors to enter premises if there is reason to believe it necessary; and to examine and investigate, to take measurements, photographs, recordings and samples and to inspect and take copies of documents.

The new powers introduced by the 1974 Act are powers to issue enforcement notices. Enforcement notices are of two kinds: improvement notices and prohibition notices. Improvement notices require the remedy of breaches of the statutory provision in question. Prohibition notices may be served where there is a risk of serious personal injury. Where such risk is imminent, the notice may be imposed with immediate effect. Otherwise it may take effect after a specified period. The prohibition is directed against the carrying on of activities in contravention of the relevant statutory provision. Such enforcement powers in respect of 'relevant statutory provisions' include provisions of the Factories Act 1961 and the Offices, Shops and Railway Premises Act 1963, as well as regulations made under them, in addition to the duties imposed by the Health and Safety at Work Act itself.

Section 33 of the Health and Safety at Work provides for the ultimate sanction of criminal penalties. As noted earlier in connection with individual employees, it is an offence (applicable to everyone, employer and employee alike) to fail to discharge a positive duty imposed or accepted under the terms of the Act in respect of health and safety, and intentionally or recklessly to interfere with or misuse anything provided in the interests of health, safety or welfare in pursuance of any relevant statutory provision. Just as the enforcement powers in respect of improvement and prohibition notices apply in the case of the factories and offices legislation as well as to duties under the 1974 Act itself, so also do the powers of criminal prosecution contained in the 1974 Act. To complement the new enforcement notices introduced by the 1974 Act, section 33(1)(g) provides that it is an offence 'to contravene any requirement or prohibition imposed by an improvement notice or a prohibition notice.'

Owing to the legal position of the Crown (see p. 19), National Health Service hospitals and other premises do not attract the 1974 Act's powers of enforcement in the ordinary way. Under section 20, noted above, inspectors may enter National Health Service premises and carry out their inspection and associated functions. But prosecutions for criminal offences under safety legislation cannot be brought against the Crown.

If, therefore, a Crown improvement notice is issued against a health authority, it will be morally but not legally binding. Disobedience or failure to implement the effect of the notice cannot be prosecuted as a criminal offence. Individual employees may, however, be prosecuted if necessary. Such a prosecution might be brought, for instance, for an offence under section 7 or section 8 of the 1974 Act, noted earlier. The Health and Safety Executive will not, as a matter of practice, prosecute an employee merely as a substitute for the health authority which it cannot prosecute. Prosecutions are brought against health authority employees only in cases where they would have been brought against employees of bodies not protected by this legal exemption or privilege.

Approved Codes of Practice

A principal objective of the Health and Safety at Work Act 1974 is the unifying and streamlining of standards and enforcement processes. In addition to new enforcement powers in respect of improvement and prohibition, a further important innovation is the statutory backing given under section 16 of the Act to approved codes of practice. Few such codes have been issued, though a code under consideration at the time of writing will have important effects on the practices of radiography and radiotherapy.

Above the Health and Safety Executive, which is the tier of authority charged with the duty of enforcement of health and safety standards, is the Health and Safety Commission. An important practical function of the Commission is the approval and issue (whether or not prepared by itself) of codes of practice. The purpose of such codes is to provide detailed practical guidance on the provisions and requirements, in a particular area, set out in sections 2 to 7 of the 1974 Act itself. Some of these were noted earlier. Codes are envisaged as providing practical guidance to any existing statutory provision, including the legislation relating to factories and offices.

The consent of the Secretary of State is a requirement for a code to be approved. And before seeking the consent of the Secretary of State the Commission shall consult any relevant government department or other body which appears to the Commission to be appropriate. Of special note to those engaged in the practices of radiotherapy and radiography is the fact that section 16 itself refers to consultation, in the case of a code relating to electromagnetic radiations, with the National Radiological Protection Board. The Act requires the Board to be consulted in the case of any such code. As mentioned in a moment, this very process is taking place at the time of writing.

It is natural that the consent of the Secretary of State should be required for the approval of a code of practice under the Act. Such codes will in many instances be filling out the practical details of health and safety requirements in a way similar to that which would be adopted in regulations. And regulations are, typically, made by government departments under powers conferred by statute.

Under section 17 of the 1974 Act, a failure to observe the requirements of an approved code of practice will not of itself give rise to criminal or civil proceedings. In this respect the requirements of approved codes differ from those of regulations, non-compliance with which may itself be an offence under section 33 of the 1974 Act (mentioned earlier).

Such a failure or omission is nevertheless admissible as evidence in criminal proceedings for contravention of any specific legal provision in respect of which there exists an approved code of practice. (Effects on civil liability are considered on page 101.) Furthermore, breach of any provision of a code which a court considers relevant to proof of breach of a statutory requirement or prohibition will normally be taken as proof of such breach. An exception is made where the court is satisfied that compliance was made otherwise than by the observance of the relevant code of practice.

Further down in the legal hierarchy of safety requirements and advice come guidance notes, issued normally by the Health and Safety Commission or the Health and Safety Executive in connection with regulations, or a code of practice, or both.

CIVIL ACTION CONCERNING HEALTH AND SAFETY

The legal principles according to which a civil action for damages by an injured person may be based on the breach, possibly by an employer, of a duty imposed by a statute or regulation have been discussed. It remains briefly to consider the position of an injured individual in connection with breach of health and safety regulations imposed by the 1974 Act and regulations made under it.

It will be recalled that sections 2 to 7 of the Health and Safety at Work Act impose 'general duties' in respect of health and safety, some of which were noted; and that section 8 prohibits misuse of equipment and misconduct, if intentional or reckless. While breach of these provisions will, as has also been noted, give rise to criminal proceedings, in which the requirements of approved codes of practice may also provide relevant evidence, section 47(1) of the Act makes a clear distinction between such criminal matters, and civil actions.

Section 47(1) provides that nothing in the Act shall be construed as conferring upon an injured individual a civil action in respect of failure to comply with duties under sections 2 to 7 or of a contravention of section 8. As to the position under *regulations*, as distinct from under the statute itself, a division must be drawn between regulations made under other statutes, namely legislation relating to factories and offices, and those made and to be made under the Health and Safety at Work Act itself.

In the case of the former, civil actionability continues to depend on the wording of each individual regulation, and on the rules relating to breach of statutory duty (discussed earlier in this chapter) if the regulations are not explicit one way or the other on civil liability. But in the case of regulations made and to be made under the 1974 Act section 47(2) states that, unless otherwise provided in the regulation, breach of a duty which it imposes is to be civilly actionable. As in the case of any action for breach of a statutory duty, injury must be proved.

Furthermore, section 47(5) invalidates any agreement purporting to exclude or restrict the effect of section 47(2), namely that civil liability exists under health and safety regulations, unless such exclusion or restriction is expressly permitted by the regulations in question. It remains to be seen what use, if any, will be made of this exceptional exclusionary power. It should be noted that, even if a particular regulation excludes civil liability arising from its breach, an injured person may still bring an ordinary action in negligence. Proof of damage, in the sense of injury, is again essential to the success of such an action.

Failure to observe the requirements of an approved code of practice will not of itself give rise to any civil proceedings. However, the effect, under section 17 of the Health and Safety at Work Act, on criminal liability was noted earlier. And a criminal conviction is, furthermore, admissible under section 11(1) of the Civil Evidence Act 1968 as evidence, in subsequent civil proceedings that the offence was committed. In civil proceedings for injury resulting from breach of the requirement of an approved code of practice, such evidence is likely to assist the plaintiff's action for damages.

Moreover, since the requirements of an approved code result from approved practice in the field to which they relate, non-observance may in any case be regarded as evidence of negligence. There is no doubt, also, that voluntary codes other than statutorily approved codes will provide similar evidence in appropriate cases. If the requirements of a voluntary code resemble or coincide with requirements contained in an approved code for what is in fact a different area or field, the voluntary code's requirements are that much more likely to be taken as the basis of a negligence claim in the event of their breach.

INJURY COMPENSATION FROM SOCIAL SECURITY

It is not within the scope of this book to give any but the briefest detail on the award of compensation from social security sources. The principle of state insurance compensation should, however, be included in the overall picture of redress for injuries at work. Such state insurance compensation is independent of proof of fault or liability in any person towards the victim of the injury. It therefore affords yet a further avenue of injury redress in addition to those already discussed.

The Social Security Act 1975 provides for the payment of social security benefit in respect of industrial injuries. Section 50 provides for benefit to be payable to an employed earner in respect of personal injury by accident 'arising out of or in the course of his employment'.

The benefits so payable in respect of industrial injury were until 1983 industrial injury benefit, disablement benefit and, in the case of fatalities at work, industrial death benefit. Industrial injury benefit was abolished by section 39 of the Social Security and Housing Benefits Act 1982. In many cases the difference, if any, between sickness benefit, payable for the fact of being off work through sickness, and industrial injury benefit had become negligible. Disablement benefit is now payable no earlier than 90 days after the accident which caused the disability, even though the claimant may be physically capable of returning to work before that date.

The matter now requiring discussion is the meaning of the ingredients of the expression 'personal injury . . . by accident arising out of or in' the course of employment. The personal injury may include both physical and mental injury. Mental injury may manifest itself in a psychosomatic form, like nervous shock or depression, or it may even amount to actual mental impairment.

The injury for which a claim is made must have been caused by an 'accident'. For this purpose an accident has been held to include a deliberately wrongful act as well as a negligent injury or just a mishap. The House of Lords ruled in respect of earlier relevant legislation in *Fenton v. Thorley and Co. Ltd.* (1903) that an accident is an 'untoward event' which is not expected or designed. Thus a therapist or other practitioner attacked by a patient would suffer an 'accident' in this sense.

An 'accident' may also extend to cover an irregular series of events over some period of time, and in this regard an 'accident' is to be distinguished from a 'process'. Benefit in respect of industrial injury is available for harm caused by an accident, as defined above, but not generally in consequence of a 'process'. Injury or disease resulting from a process may, as noted below, be compensated if it falls within the harm recognised as being inherent in one of a specific number of industrial conditions or diseases which are separately specified in regulations.

To be an injury arising 'out of or in the course of employment' it is not essential that the employee was actually doing the job he or she was employed to do at the time of the accident. Injuries occurring during meal breaks and during the time of preparing to start or finish work are also included. A person is 'at work' and 'in the course of employment' when on the employer's premises. It seems probable also that a practitioner on the way to visit a patient at the patient's home will be 'in the course of employment' while travelling there and while returning to the hospital, health centre, practice or whatever.

In *R. v. National Insurance Commissioner, ex parte Michael* (1977) a policeman made a claim in respect of injuries received while playing football for his local police force. However, even though such sporting activities were encouraged it was held that the injury did not arise in the course of employment. A case in which a therapist received injury while engaging in recognised and proper sporting or similar activity with patients would, by contrast, be almost certain to be decided in the therapist's favour. What is required is that the activity in question must be 'reasonably incidental' to the job the claimant is employed to do. In the case of the therapist in this example, reasonable and accepted practice within the profession will play an important if not decisive role in such a claim.

While the rulings just discussed follow from decisions in individual cases, four specific situations are provided for by the Social Security Act itself. First, an accident is deemed to arise out of the course of employment even if at the time it happened the claimant was acting in contravention of employer's instructions or of a statutory provision or regulations. That is, provided the accident would have been deemed to have arisen apart from the contravention, and provided the act in question was done for the purposes of and in connection with the employer's business (s. 52).

Second, an accident is deemed to arise out of and in the course of employment if at the time the employee was travelling to or from work as a passenger (not as a driver) in a vehicle operated by or on behalf of his employer and not operated in the ordinary course of a public transport service (s. 53). Third, an accident is deemed so to arise when an employee is taking steps to meet an emergency, actual or supposed. The emergency action must be taken, and the accident thus occur, 'in or about any premises at which he is for the time being employed for the purpose of his employer's trade or business'; and the employee must be 'taking steps, on an actual or supposed emergency at those premises, to rescue, succour or protect persons who are, or are thought to be or possibly to be, injured or imperilled, or to avert or minimise serious damage to property' (s. 54).

Fourthly, an accident is so treated if it arises in the course of the claimant's employment and is caused by another person's 'misconduct, skylarking or negligence'. Such other person need not be a fellow-employee, but could be a patient also. Section 55, which provides for such misconduct, skylarking or negligence, makes the same provision in the case of the behaviour or presence of any animal, and in the case of the claimant's being struck by lightning. It is a condition of entitlement under this section that 'the employee did not directly or indirectly induce or contribute to the happening of the accident by his conduct outside the employment or by any act not incidental to the employment'.

Prescribed diseases

While some diseases contracted at work might be contracted in such a way as to fall within the definition of an 'accident', many will arise due to a gradual or regular 'process' and thus fall outside the rules so far considered. Section 76 of the Social Security Act 1975 therefore enables the Secretary of State to prescribe certain diseases and injuries as entitling a claimant to benefit.

The risk must be a risk of the occupation and not a risk common to everyone whether or not engaged in the job in question. The disease or injury must also be such that its attribution to the nature of the employment can normally be established with reasonable certainty.

One such disease is tuberculosis. Practitioners in every one of the professions supplementary to medicine might fall within the prescription relating to tuberculosis, but especially remedial therapists in close contact with infirm patients, and medical laboratory scientific officers working with material which is a source of tuberculosis infection. Another prescribed disease for social security purposes is viral hepatitis. This disease is prescribed in respect of any occupation involving close and frequent contact with human blood, or close and frequent contact with a source of viral hepatitis infection by reason of employment in a service ancillary to medical treatment or nursing of a person suffering from viral hepatitis.

A further prescribed disease is inflammation, ulceration or malignant disease of the skin or subcutaneous tissues due to electromagnetic radiations (other than radiant heat) or to ionising particles. While radiographers engaged in diagnostic work would hardly be likely, except through bad and constant careless use of equipment, to suffer the prescribed injury so defined, it could apply in the case of radiographers engaged in radiotherapy treatment on patients.

These are but a few examples, chosen for their particular relevance to certain professions supplementary to medicine. The full list of prescribed diseases and injuries is long. Details will be found in the Social Security (Industrial Injuries) (Prescribed Diseases) Regulations 1980.[3]

REFERENCES

[1] Circular DS 166/71
[2] S.I. 1974 No. 1681
[3] S.I. 1980 No. 377

Chapter Seven

NEGLIGENCE

ELEMENTS OF NEGLIGENCE

It is not every accident or mishap which will result in the legal liability of a person doing or omitting to do something, even if injury or harm ensues. An action for damages against someone alleged to have been responsible for an injury requires proof of the breach of a legal duty. Some duties are imposed by statute. But the majority of duties relevant to the law of negligence owe their origin and development to the common law established through decided cases.

By no means every single instance of legal liability will have been considered by the courts. One reason is the obvious one that fresh instances of foolhardiness and misfortune are apt to arise every minute of each day. The other reason is that judicial decisions represent the determination of disputed cases. If, therefore, a particular instance of possible legal liability has not presented itself before the courts in the form of a dispute, no opportunity will have arisen for a ruling to be made on it.

The three essential ingredients of negligence are duty, breach and damage. A negligent injury, for instance to a patient or to a colleague, consists of an injury caused by the breach of a duty of care. As will be shown, all three elements must be proved if an action for damages is to succeed.

Duty of care

It is elementary that a duty of care is owed by paramedical practitioners to those whom they undertake to treat or to whom they undertake some other professional responsibility appropriate to their particular profession. The particular incidence of the duty may vary as between the professions: physiotherapists, orthoptists, chiropodists, dietitians, remedial gymnasts and occupational therapists all engage in patient or client treatment, though restrictions are in some cases imposed by scope rules in the case of registered practitioners. Radiographers and medical laboratory scientific officers are, on the other hand, forbidden by their scope rules to hold themselves out as professionally qualified to diagnose or treat disease. These two professions nevertheless owe a legal duty of care to those in respect of whom they conduct their investigations.

A matter which is not so obvious but which is sometimes important in practice is the time at which such a duty arises. Paramedical practitioners are not, any more than any other person, legally obliged to exercise their own particular skills in the assistance of someone with whom they have no connection. If, for instance, a practitioner happens to witness an accident there might be some assistance which could usefully be given to an injured person on the basis of special skill and knowledge. But the law imposes no positive duty to act in such a case, and no legal wrong is done by leaving an injured person unattended, even if greater harm or suffering is caused as a result. If assistance is given, however, the person rendering assistance may become legally liable if improper attention causes injury or greater injury. Mr Justice Willes said in the case of *Skelton v. London North Western Railway* (1867):

> If a person undertakes to perform a voluntary act he is liable if he performs it improperly, but not if he neglects to perform it.

If assistance is rendered, the good Samaritan giving it will be assessed in the light of the particular situation. For instance, help given in an emergency will be assessed in the light of prevailing conditions, which may well prevent even a skilled and experienced person from spotting a possible dangerous feature of a situation, for instance an allergy, in the injured person.

In the case of paramedical practitioners to whom patients are referred by medical or dental practitioners, a duty of care to the patient will arise once the patient is accepted and treatment undertaken. Questions of delay in treatment may well give rise to a breach of duty (a question considered below) once responsibility for a patient's treatment has been undertaken. In a hospital or clinic, or in a general practice employing a paramedical practitioner, the time treatment is undertaken is the time which treatment starts. So if, for instance, a doctor were to treat or diagnose a patient and then refer that patient for further attention, the therapist would be unable to claim a reason for delay which might legitimately be claimed by a private practitioner who delays treatment simply until an appointment becomes vacant. The arrangements in the hospital, clinic or practice are required, once the treatment of the patient is undertaken, to proceed with reasonable speed and efficiency.

If, as would be the normal explanation of any such delay within the system, the fault lay in the organisation itself, liability for injury or (more likely) further suffering would attach to the hospital, clinic or practice in the form of primary liability. The reader is referred to page 70 for an explanation of the way in which the law casts liability for a system directly on the organisation or institution responsible for that system.

It is just conceivable that a therapist in private practice to whom a patient is referred by a doctor or dentist might be regarded as negligent in delaying an appointment with a patient whom the therapist knew or ought to have known was in urgent need of treatment. Much would in practice depend on the sufficiency of information supplied by the referring practitioner, who might also in certain circumstances be negligent. A more credible form of negligence in a private practitioner therapist would be an unreasonable delay between appointments in the case of someone whose condition clearly required more frequent treatment than that which was given.

The legal duty of care which constitutes the first of the three essentials of negligence is owed irrespective of any contract between the practitioner and the patient or client. In the absence of an agreement between practitioner and patient or client, which forms an obvious connection between the parties, that connection is formed for the purposes of the law of negligence by the notion of duty of care. As to what that duty requires, we need to turn to cases in which courts have asked whether a breach of duty has occurred. That we do in the following section.

But, contract apart, there is no legal duty to effect a cure. The legal requisites of care sufficient to avoid an allegation of negligence irrespective of contract are those of taking such measures as are reasonable in the case of a reasonably competent practitioner of the class in question, and of avoiding such acts as such a practitioner would avoid. If there is, as there will be in private practice, a contractual relationship between practitioner and client, it is legally possible for the contract to guarantee a cure. It would be an unwise practitioner who would go so far as to give guarantees, however. Even in contract, the legal duty is normally to treat the client with reasonable skill and competence.

Breach of the duty of care

Once the legal connection between practitioner and patient or client has been made by way of the notion of 'duty of care', the second ingredient of negligence, namely breach of duty, falls to be considered. Terminology now changes and instead of duty of care we need to talk in terms of the standard of care required if negligence is to be avoided. Just as there is no special type of negligence which is called 'medical negligence', only negligence as committed by medical practitioners, neither is there any special type of negligence called 'paramedical negligence'. It is, again, simply a breach of the duty of care required of paramedical practitioners. It follows, therefore, that the principles of negligence applicable to any skilled professional practice are relevant to a discussion of the legal responsibility of paramedical practitioners. At the same time, nevertheless, it will be convenient to take most of the necessary illustrations from the field of medical practice since the situations involving allegations of want of reasonable care by paramedicals are often closely akin to those encountered in medical practice itself.

The word 'reasonable' recurs constantly in any discussion of the care requisite to the fulfilment of the legal duty to a patient. There are two respects in which the idea of reasonableness is important in any specialist field, including those relevant to this book. On the one hand, the requisite standard of care could not conceivably mean the standard achieved by the very best practitioner in the field in question. There is only one such person, and even then probably for only one particular moment. Reasonable competence is clearly below the best that can be expected.

On the other hand, reasonable competence demands more than anyone's own particular best, or their own particular best at any given moment. A practitioner who feels tired or ill must still measure up to the standard of reasonable competence and skill to be expected of a practitioner of that type or class. The case of *Barnett v. Chelsea and Kensington HMC* (1968) involved the inaction of a hospital doctor who was himself feeling ill. Some night watchmen had somehow become poisoned by arsenic in their tea, and they went to the local hospital for treatment. The doctor, whom the court considered responsible for attending to these men when they presented themselves, told a nurse who telephoned him from the casualty department that he was ill himself and had been vomiting. He instructed the nurse to tell the men to go home and to call in their own doctors. Though the doctor and the health authority escaped liability the court held that in failing to admit and treat one of the night watchmen, who later died, the doctor as casualty officer had failed to discharge his duty of care and was therefore negligent.

One of the most frequently cited tests for deciding whether or not there has been a breach of duty is the statement of Baron Alderson in *Blyth v. Birmingham Waterworks Co.* (1856):

> Negligence is the omission to do something which a reasonable man, guided upon those considerations which ordinarily regulate the conduct of human affairs, would do, or doing something which a prudent and reasonable man would not do.

But in the case of skilled professionals, including paramedical practitioners, the requisite standard of care expected if a breach of duty is to be avoided must be more specifically expressed. Speaking of the standard of care expected of a surgeon, but using a description applicable equally to paramedical practitioners, Lord Justice Scott said in *Mahon v. Osborne* (1939):

> . . . it is desirable to recall the well-established legal measure of a professional man's duty. If he professes an art he must be reasonably skilled in it. There is no doubt that the defendant surgeon was that. He must also be careful, but the standard of care the law requires is not insurance against accidental slips. It is such a degree of care as a normally skilful member of the profession may reasonably be expected to exercise in the circumstances of the case in question. It is not every slip or mistake which imports negligence ...[1]

Lord Justice Scott was referring in that case to the standard of care expected of a surgeon, simply because it was a surgeon whose actions were in question in the particular dispute. The principle of responsibility is equally applicable throughout the specialties practised in the professions supplementary to medicine. In the case of *Gold v. Essex County Council* (1942) it was the alleged negligence of a radiographer which resulted in injury to the plaintiff.

The plaintiff was a five-year-old girl who was taken to hospital for the treatment of warts on her face. The visiting dermatologist ordered treatment by 1000 units of Grenz rays and sent the girl to the radiology department with a written note of the treatment she should receive there. The department was in the charge of a radiologist but the treatment was given to the girl by a qualified and competent radiographer. During treatment the girl's face was covered with a lead-lined rubber cloth which protected all but the affected part of her face.

The warts did not yield to this treatment and so the dermatologist ordered the number of units of rays to be doubled. During the next treatment session the radiographer covered the girl's face with a piece of lint only and as a result the girl's face was permanently disfigured. This was such a lack of care as fell below the standard expected of a reasonably competent radiographer, and in this case negligence on his part was admitted.

Specific questions arising from the standard of care expected from paramedical practitioners, and the consequent question of breach of duty of care, will be examined after the following discussion of the third vital element of negligence. That element is the damage, harm or injury which must be proved to have resulted from the carelessness which constitutes the breach of duty.

The resulting damage

An act of carelessness, or at least an act which falls below the standard of care reasonably to be expected of the class of practitioner in question, will not give rise to an action in negligence unless it is proved that the breach of duty caused damage or injury. The damage may consist of personal injury, damage to property or financial loss. What the law calls 'nervous shock' is included within the category of physical injury provided the results manifest themselves in the form of symptoms such as nausea, a rash or a depressive neurosis – unless there is a contract, in which case damages for worry and upset may be included in the damages awarded for breach of contract. The law of negligence will not compensate 'mere' worry, upset or grief falling short of the physical symptoms manifesting themselves in the form of 'nervous shock'. Even in the case of breach of contract the worry and upset must, if it is to be compensated by way of inclusion in the damages, be a foreseeable result of the breach.

To say that an action for damages will not succeed unless the breach of duty can be established as the cause of the damage or injury is not, of course, to say that such carelessness will have no consequences in other directions. On the contrary, serious cases of careless treatment may come within the definition of serious professional misconduct (p. 45) and therefore will fall within the jurisdiction of the disciplinary committee of the relevant board within the statutory structure. A simple serious act of carelessness endangering another, or a series of careless acts, may lead to disciplinary action by an employer or employing authority. In very serious cases it could, subject to the rules and principles of fairness of dismissal (p. 63), lead to dismissal from post.

A particular instance of the possibility of professional disciplinary action even without proof that a practitioner actually injured a patient or client, and even in the absence of proof of any breach of the duty of care, is that of a paramedical practitioner acting outside the 'scope rules' relevant to his or her particular profession. As an example, the scope of practice of registered physiotherapists is defined in statement of infamous conduct thus: 'A physiotherapist should confine him/herself to treatment in those fields of physiotherapy in which he/she has been trained.'

If no damage or injury resulted from an action taken outside the scope rules, negligence would not be committed. Even if some harm were actually to befall a patient or client as a result of actions falling outside the scope rules, actionable negligence would not necessarily be proved against the practitioner in question. It would still have to be proved that the practitioner fell below the standard of care reasonably to be expected of a competent practitioner giving the treatment in question. However, if damage or injury were to result from an act done outside the practitioner's own field of training, the burden of proof would easily be shifted by the plaintiff on to the practitioner. The latter might in such circumstances find it very difficult to prove that reasonable care had been taken to act with the competence of a practitioner who was in fact trained in the field in question.

Experienced and trainee practitioners

It is in the nature of experience that some qualified paramedical practitioners are more experienced and perhaps by that token also more skilled than others. The standard of care expected by the law is simply that of the reasonably competent practitioner of the particular class in question, measured in respect of the field of activity for which the practitioner in question assumes responsibility. It was mentioned above that a paramedical practitioner who undertakes treatment or other responsibility to a patient or client which is outside the scope rules relevant to that practitioner may find it difficult to discharge the burden of proof if an allegation of negligence is made. Even in the case of an experienced practitioner, actions beyond that person's normal scope of practice may be held negligent. To do so he has to fall below the standard of care expected of a competent practitioner in that field in which responsibility is undertaken. Even a practitioner experienced and skilled in one field may exhibit want of reasonable care outside that field. It is no more an answer to say in this instance that the practitioner was doing his best in that further field of activity, than it is to say he was doing his tired or incompetent best in the normal field of practice.

An exception to this general principle relating to the law's requirement of competence in the field of treatment or other responsibility undertaken exists in the case of emergencies. Provided the emergency was not of the practitioner's own creation, a degree of care and skill would be required which was appropriate in the circumstances. In an emergency the normal scope or field of practice would be that much less likely to count against the hard-pressed practitioner in question, if the emergency required treatment outside that field.

The position of students or trainees is somewhat similar, except that in their case the question of standard of care is likely to arise not so much from doing something outside a particular field, but rather from doing anything which a qualified practitioner would do within the scope or field for which training is being given.

Both qualified and trainee or students are judged according to the skill and competence they hold themselves out as possessing. Consequently, emergencies apart, trainees and students who undertake a responsibility which is in fact beyond their competence place themselves in a difficult position. For the legal measure or standard of care expected of them is that of a competent practitioner who would normally undertake that sort of responsibility.

So much for a case in which a student or trainee voluntarily undertakes responsibility for treatment which is beyond his or her competence. But what of a case in which the trainee has received instructions from a trainer or other superior member of staff to do the very act which causes the plaintiff patient's injury?

Acting on instructions

As a general proposition of law it can be said that a trainee or student has a duty to carry out the instructions of an instructor or superior, unless those instructions are manifestly wrong. The same principle applies to instructions given to qualified but still junior practitioners who receive instructions from a more senior colleague in the hierarchy. The case which establishes this principle in fact involved the latter kind of relationship.

In *Junor v. McNicol* (1959) a boy lost his arm as a result of inadequate hospital treatment followed by premature discharge from hospital. The house surgeon in immediate charge of the boy's treatment had not in fact, on the evidence which was accepted, heard the whole of the consultant's instructions to her. He had ordered three days' penicillin treatment, but the house surgeon did not hear this instruction. She nevertheless gave some penicillin treatment, of her own motion, even though the discharge from hospital was too early. She had in fact followed what she, on the evidence, believed her instructions to be. It was not, the court held, one of those cases in which she should have disregarded her instructions (or her instructions as she believed them to be) as being manifestly wrong. Nevertheless the House of Lords did nothing to question decisions which establish that, where instructions from a superior are manifestly wrong, both legal duty and common sense dictate that they should not be followed.

Even, however, if a student or a junior staff member were to be held personally liable for an act beyond his or her competence causing injury to a patient and the order was manifestly wrong, it seems fairly certain that if the employer or employing authority were a co-defendant to the injured patient's action, the junior or trainee would be fully indemnified. In a case in which the superior order was not manifestly wrong but was given as a result of the negligence of the instructor or superior colleague, it should be the latter who would be the defendant in an action by the patient for damages and not the trainee or junior. Apparently correct and reasonable instructions appear themselves to condition the sphere of competence of trainees and juniors.

Supervisory duties of instructors

The standard of care expected of the instructor himself or herself is that which is sufficient in all the circumstances of the teaching situation, and later developments of it, to avoid foreseeable injury to trainees themselves, to those they are treating, and to those they may treat when they have left the classroom and are practising in, say, another part of the hospital. The opportunities for legal liability of an instructor fall into two main divisions. First, where instructions are given directly to a trainee to do a certain act or to handle a patient (if there is one in the particular training situation) in a certain way. Second, where a negligent instruction is given to a trainee who subsequently and in later practice acts on the instruction to his or her detriment or to that of a patient.

As for negligent instructions in the classroom or learning field, an instructor owes a duty to trainee and to patient not to make a careless statement which would foreseeably cause physical injury or harm to either. So far as injury to a trainee is concerned, the words of Lord Justice Slesser in the case of *Sharp v. Avery* (1938) [2] are instructive. He said:

> . . . when one person by his conduct invites another to rely upon his skill to do something which he otherwise might not do, after that, he may owe a duty to the person whom he has invited to place reliance upon him, and may be liable if he fails in the skill which he represented that he possessed, and in reliance on which the other man altered his course of conduct.

Though these words related to the particular case before the court in which one motorcyclist had acted in reliance on the knowledge of the road which the defendant motorcyclist said he possessed, and was injured by the latter's negligent guidance, the principle of the case seems equally applicable to a three-party situation in which the person injured is not the trainee but the patient.

So far as future liability to patients or to practitioners themselves once they have left the training situation is concerned, the same principle appears to apply. If injury to either were to be held to be a foreseeable consequence of the original negligent instruction, then the person who gave it would be liable to be sued for negligence by the person injured. The case of *Clayton v. Woodman and Son (Builders) Ltd.* (1962) is authority for the proposition that liability for personal injury may result from careless instructions which the person issuing them knew would be obeyed. The facts of the case, involving negligent instructions by an architect to a bricklayer causing injury to the latter, in fact involved an instruction which the person giving it ought to have known would be promptly obeyed.

There seems, however, no reason to believe that a court would not, in a suitable case, be prepared to impose liability for a negligent instruction even if it was acted upon to the practitioner's or the patient's detriment after it was originally given. It should be added, though, that different considerations might become relevant if some time had elapsed in the interim. The question might arise as to whether there had been, in that period, any circumstances which ought to have made the person acting upon the original negligent instruction know that it was in fact erroneous. If anything which had happened in the interim ought to have made the recipient of the instruction aware of the error it contained, the chain of causation between the instruction and the injury would be regarded as broken. If injury befell a patient in consequence, the action would then lie against the practitioner who caused it.

Lest this result seem inconsistent with the principle explained above in relation to the case of *Junor v. McNicol* (1959), it should be pointed out that the junior doctor in that case was acting directly on the instructions of a superior, given in respect of a particular case. The instance now being considered, however, is one in which some period of time elapses in which the recipient of the instruction may have an opportunity to check its correctness.

In addition to taking care not to give carelessly incorrect instructions themselves, instructors and trainers also owe a duty to maintain such supervision over the learning period and over all those involved in it as is reasonably sufficient to prevent harm or injury to any such person. This duty in respect of the system of instruction which is pursued is a duty which is shared also by the employing authority, if there is one. So far as injury to its staff is concerned, whether to instructor or trainee, an employer or employing authority owes those duties to establish and maintain a safe system of work which were examined in Chapter 5. So far as patients or other third parties to the employment relationship are concerned, not only may the employer be vicariously liable (p. 67) for the faults of an employee but also (Chapter 5, p. 83) primarily liable in respect of an inadequate system of training supervision.

The supervisory responsibilities of an instructor do not end at the classroom door or at the end of training. It is therefore advisable for the system in any organisation, say a hospital, to provide for communication between the classroom instructor and the clinical supervisor or other such responsible person as to the trainees' competence and knowledge as they pass out of the learning situation. Again, the primary responsibility for effecting such communication lies with those operating the organisation (say a hospital) as a whole.

SUPERVISION AND SPECIAL RISKS

A general duty to maintain adequate supervision is owed by those in charge of others who may foreseeably be injured if reasonable care is not taken for their safety. The particular responsibilities of an instructor have just been examined. But on a wider front, supervisory duties may be owed by practitioners to anyone who may foreseeably be injured if surveillance is not maintained. Among such situations are included those in which the particular patient presents special risks, and requires supervision for that reason. Mental patients may be a case in point. For instance, occupational therapists involved with the mentally disordered owe a duty both to them and to others to avoid injury or harm.

In *Selfe v. Ilford and District HMC* (1970) the plaintiff was a psychiatric patient and a known suicide risk. While unsupervised he left his bed, climbed onto a roof, threw himself off and received severe injuries. The hospital and its staff were held liable for negligence for failing to provide the necessary continuous supervision which the patient needed. The fact that the injuries were self-inflicted made no difference to the responsibility of the defendants. Their duty was to take such care as in all the circumstances was reasonably sufficient for the plaintiff patient's protection.

This supervisory and surveillance duty is not, however, without its practical limitations, as illustrated in the case of *Thorne v. Northern Group HMC* (1964). In an action by the husband of a woman who had left hospital to return home, where she committed suicide, the defendants were held not to have failed in their duty to maintain adequate supervision. Lord Justice Edmund Davies said:

> As later events showed, the patient was set upon making her escape for the purpose of self-destruction, and it was highly conceivable that she kept a wary eye on the nurses and seized her opportunity immediately their backs were turned and they had absented themselves temporarily. That did not connote negligence on the part of the nurses.

And in *Hyde v. Tameside AHA* (1981) the Court of Appeal reversed a judgement awarding £200,000 damages to a man who attempted suicide and received massive injuries in consequence. There had been nothing in the patient's behaviour to put staff on enquiry or to alert them directly to the possibility of a suicide attempt. It would be wrong, said the appeal judges, to found liability on a chain of causation which depended only on a series of possibilities.

FAILURE OF COMMUNICATION

It is not only an error in the process of treatment itself which may lead to liability in negligence. Poor communications may themselves cause erroneous or at least inadequate action to be taken on their basis. The case of *Junor v. McNicol*, examined above, was a case in which a partially-heard instruction did not in the event lead to a finding of negligence. The allegation in that case was brought against the junior house surgeon who, on the evidence, acted on the part of the consultant's instruction which she heard. It was not a case in which any negligence was alleged in the consultant himself.

Duties to ensure proper and adequate communications exist as between referring GPs or hospital doctors and the receiving paramedical practitioners, for instance physiotherapists. Likewise the paramedical practitioner may, in the circumstances of a particular case, be under a duty to make sure the referring doctor is given any necessary information about the patient. The response of a particular patient to the therapy recommended by the doctor and given by the physiotherapist would be required if the referring doctor asks for it, probably with a view to the future handling and treatment of the patient in question. There will also, in accordance with prevailing professional practice, be certain obligations on the therapist to communicate with the referring doctor or another practitioner who has a legitimate interest in the treatment of the patient.

It would be idle to speculate upon particular instances in which specific duties of communication with a referring or other practitioner exist. What can be said, by way of general principle, is that the approved and general practice within the profession or professions involved in a particular case will be greatly influential on the outcome of any allegation of want of reasonable care.

The courts will not allow themselves to be bound by the fact that a particular way of doing things is generally approved as acceptable practice within a particular profession. It might happen, though in practice only on very rare occasions, that a practice approved in a profession itself fell below a standard acceptable to the law. Nevertheless, expert professional evidence that a certain form of conduct is generally accepted will be strong evidence that the requisite standard of care has been fulfilled.

It would be less reasonable, in considering whether or not the requisite standard of care had been fulfilled, to relay instructions and messages via a very young or very old patient than it would be to do so through an adult. Even in the case of adult patients, particular care should be taken in relation to mentally disordered and especially mentally retarded patients, with whom many therapists come into contact as part of their professional responsibilities.

DELEGATION OF TREATMENT

It may in some cases be reasonable to delegate treatment or monitoring to the patient or someone in the patient's household when treatment is being given on a domiciliary basis. Great care must be taken in the aspects of a patient's treatment and management which can properly be delegated, for two reasons. First, an improper delegation leading to injury to the patient or to a member of the household engaged in the delegated treatment will constitute negligence. Second, improper delegation amounts to an abrogation of professional duties and would therefore be likely to lead to disciplinary proceedings for professional misconduct.

Even where delegation of an aspect of patient care or treatment is in itself proper, it is essential that adequate instructions are given by the practitioner to the patient or his attendant or relative. In giving such instructions to the person whom the practitioner intends should act upon them, it must again be borne in mind that some patients, or those looking after them, may lack a full or adequate understanding of the instructions. In the case of a patient or attendant who is mentally retarded, indications are against any but the most basic of instructions on matters to be left to the person in question. In such a case, anything which formed part of a treatment process as distinct from processes incidental to normal family and domiciliary care would be most unwisely delegated.

In other cases of limited understanding the appropriateness and the wisdom of delegating any part of a treatment process will depend upon a number of factors. These include, principally, the nature and effects of the treatment and of the aspect of it which is delegated, the adequacy of the instructions given by the practitioner, the understanding of the person to whom the instructions are given, and the extent to which that understanding was or ought to have been checked by the practitioner.

A decided case involving the delegation of an aspect of treatment to a patient when the practitioner was still present and participating in the treatment itself is *Clarke v. Adams* (1950). The injured plaintiff was being treated by the defendant physiotherapist for a fibrositic condition of the left heel. In the process of diathermy the patient suffered burning which was so bad that the leg had to be amputated below the knee. Before applying the treatment the physiotherapist gave the patient the following warning: 'When I turn on the machine I want you to experience a comfortable warmth and nothing more; if you do, I want you to tell me.' Expert evidence was given by the chief examiner for the Chartered Society of Physiotherapy that the warning was entirely proper.

Mr Justice Slade said that in physiotherapy the co-operation of the patient was vital. The instrument which the physiotherapist used was dangerous because burns caused by it could lead to serious consequences. The apparatus was not in any way defective and the sole question to be decided was whether the warning given by the physiotherapist was adequate. There must in such circumstances, said the judge, be a warning of the danger as it would appear to a hypothetically reasonable person.

Would the words used here, he asked, warn such a person that his safety depended on informing the physiotherapist the moment he felt more than a comfortable warmth? The warning, he added, must make it abundantly clear that it was a warning of danger. In the circumstances of this particular case the judge was not satisfied that the warning given, although the very warning which the defendant physiotherapist had been taught to give, was adequate. For this reason he awarded the plaintiff over £3000 in respect of his severe personal injuries.

The outcome of this case lies clearly on the borderline of acceptable and unacceptable practice. It was made clear earlier in this chapter that while expert evidence as to general and approved practice will be most influential in inclining a judicial decision in a particular direction, the courts do not allow themselves to be bound by such evidence. In the case of *Clarke v. Adams*, not even evidence of what the defendant physiotherapist had been taught, or evidence from a well-qualified senior practitioner as to what was proper and accepted practice, was allowed by the judge to dictate his decision.

Given this outcome in a case in which one element of responsibility in a process of treatment was held to be inadequately delegated even when the practitioner in question was still present and in charge of the treatment, it is clear that any dangerous process will hardly ever, if indeed at all, be properly delegated in a domiciliary situation from which the practitioner is absent at the material time.

KEEPING UP TO DATE

The duty of care owed by a paramedical practitioner to a patient or client includes the duty to keep reasonably up to date with professional knowledge and techniques, by way of the normally available literature. A failure to keep informed in this way may, if it results in injury or unnecessary suffering to a patient, fall below the requisite standard of care and therefore amount to negligence.

This principle is illustrated by the decision in *Roe v. Minister of Health* (1954). The plaintiff Mr Roe was admitted to hospital for a minor operation, and he was given a spinal anaesthetic in preparation for the operation. The anaesthetic was contained in a glass ampoule, which in turn had been stored in a solution of phenol as an antiseptic precaution. The anaesthetic contained in the ampoules had in fact, unknown to anyone, become contaminated with the phenol solution as a result of microscopic cracks or molecular flaws which were not discoverable by ordinary inspection.

As a result Mr Roe became permanently paralysed from the waist down. His action for damages alleging negligence was unsuccessful. The Court of Appeal held that the state of medical knowledge as it stood at the time the accident happened did not point to any negligence in the anaesthetist or on the part of any other member of the hospital staff. Evidence advanced at the trial drew attention to a distinguished book published in 1951 which drew attention to the particular risk which had materialised in *Roe*'s case. Had the accident in question occurred at such a time following this publication as allowed practitioners to acquaint themselves with the danger there would have been no defence that the danger was unknown and unanticipated.

The accident to Mr Roe, however, occurred in 1947. Since a finding of negligence or otherwise depends on the state of knowledge within a particular field at the time an untoward event occurs, and not at the time of the trial which may (and usually will) take place some considerable time later, no negligence could be proved in the staff in this case. It was out of the question to attribute to them the prescience of four years. It was in fact, as Lord Justice Denning (as he was then) pointed out, this extraordinary accident which first disclosed the danger. Nowadays, he said, it would be negligence not to realise the danger, but it was not then.

To have decided otherwise would have been to place an unreasonable burden on the anaesthetist and other staff responsible for the storage of anaesthetics. Lord Justice Denning added that any temptation to award damages to the plaintiff in respect of his terrible injuries must be resisted. We must not, he said, condemn as negligence that which was only a misadventure.

As to how far the law imposes a duty on a practitioner to keep up to date when relevant literature is in fact available, the decision in the case of *Crawford v. Board of Governors of Charing Cross Hospital* (1953) affords a useful illustration. The plaintiff suffered permanent brachial palsy in consequence of the position in which his arm had been left during an operation during which a blood transfusion had been made to that arm. About six months prior to the operation an article had been published in *The Lancet* which alerted practitioners to the dangers of the patient's arm remaining in such a position during such an operation.

The anaesthetist, who was accused by the injured plaintiff of negligence, admitted to having seen letters in the same journal referring back to the article, but said he had not referred to it himself. It was that failure to refer back to the article which was the basis of the negligence claim against him. This contention was, however, rejected by the Court of Appeal. On the facts, a reasonably diligent practitioner might have overlooked this single piece of specialist literature recommending against a particular practice. Lord Justice Denning said:

> It would, I think, be putting too high a burden on a medical man to say that he has to read every article appearing in the current medical press; and it would be quite wrong to suggest that a medical man is negligent because he does not at once put into operation the suggestions which some contributor or other might make in a medical journal. The time may come in a particular case when a new recommendation may be so well proved and so well known and so well accepted that it should be adopted. But that was not so in this case.

The natural corollary to this statement is that there may indeed for a time be more than one acceptable school of thought in respect of a particular treatment or procedure. The duration of such a division of professional opinion may be short, or it may be for some considerable time according to the circumstances. A variation in acceptable practice and professional attitudes at the time of an untoward incident is therefore discussed next.

DIFFERING SCHOOLS OF THOUGHT

In *Crawford's* case, above, the acceptance by the court of a practice which, on the evidence, differed from that adopted or recommended by other competent practitioners in the same field of practice is an indication that the courts will be slow to rule that a new development should be entirely substituted for an earlier practice. Clearly, however, the greater the danger in a previous practice to which attention is drawn in professional literature, the less time it will take for the new recommended practice or procedure to become the only acceptable course. Nevertheless, even very strong disapproval of a practice or course of action, possibly even by certain distinguished members of the profession in question, will not necessarily dictate a verdict of negligence if damage or injury befalls a patient in consequence of its use.

An illustration of the judicial attitude to differences and variations in professional attitudes to advisable practice is found in *Bolam v. Friern Hospital Management Committee* (1957). The plaintiff was suffering from mental illness and was advised to undergo electroconvulsive therapy. He signed a consent form but was not warned about the risk of fracture which could be involved in such treatment in a tiny minority of cases – about one in ten thousand. Though no relaxant drugs were used, their use would in fact have eliminated the risk of fracture.

The treatment, which was given in 1954, resulted in disastrous consequences for the plaintiff. The electroconvulsive therapy proceeded without the use of relaxant drugs, and he sustained severe injuries to his hips and pelvis. Among those skilled in the profession and experienced in this form of therapy there were two bodies of opinion. One body of opinion had since 1953, about a year before the plaintiff's injuries were caused, favoured the use of relaxant drugs or manual control as a general practice. The other school of thought believed that the use of these drugs was attended by mortality risks and confined the use of relaxant drugs to cases in which special reasons clearly demanded them. The plaintiff's case did not fall into this category of special case.

There were equally two bodies of opinion on the question whether, if relaxant drugs were not used, manual control should be used instead. Informed and competent professional opinion differed further, on the question whether the patient should be told about the minute risk of fracture, given that he was mentally ill and that explanation of risk might well not affect his decision whether to undergo the treatment.

The plaintiff's action for damages against the hospital and the medical staff in change of his treatment was unsuccessful. In giving judgement for the defendants Mr Justice McNair explained the legal position of a practitioner who adopts one alternative practice, approved by other competent professionals, when there is in existence a school of thought which advises a different alternative:[3]

> A doctor is not guilty of negligence if he has acted in accordance with a practice accepted as proper by a responsible body of medical men skilled in that particular art. . . . Putting it the other way round, a man is not negligent, if he is acting in accordance with such a practice, merely because there is a body of opinion who would take a contrary view. At the same time, that does not mean that a medical man can obstinately and pigheadedly carry on with some old technique if it had been proved to be contrary to what is really substantially the whole of informed medical opinion.

And, referring to variations in thought and practice caused by the passage of time and the development of new techniques and attributes he added:

> Before I get to the details of the case, it is right to say this, that it is not essential for you [it was a case involving both judge and jury] to decide which of two practices is the better practice, as long as you accept that what the defendants did was in accordance with a practice accepted by responsible persons; if the result of the evidence is that you are satisfied that his practice is better than the practice spoken of on the other side, then it is really a stronger case. Finally, bear this in mind, that you are now considering whether it was negligent for certain action to be taken in August 1954, not in February 1957 [the date of the trial of the action]; and in one of the well-known cases on this topic it has been said that you must not look with 1957 spectacles at what happened in 1954.

DEVIATION FROM NORMAL TREATMENT

A similar but somewhat different question is raised in cases in which an injury is alleged to have been negligently caused on account of a deviation from accepted practice. In such a case the question is not so much whether more than one school of thought can be found among competent practitioners, as the question: did the particular treatment deviate so substantially from an accepted norm as to be negligent?

The principle applicable to such a case can be found in the Scottish case of *Hunter v. Hanley* (1955). In that case the plaintiff was being given a series of injections by her doctor. During the final injection the needle broke and the end remained embedded in the patient's hip. The plaintiff alleged that the doctor was negligent in failing to use a suitable hypodermic needle for the injection.

One of the grounds of fault alleged against the defendant doctor was that the type of needle he employed on this occasion was not strong enough, and that any doctor possessing a fair and adequate knowledge of his profession would have known this. A question therefore arose as to what was the normal and usual practice in regard to the type of needle required.

The Lord President Clyde said:[4]

> In the realm of diagnosis and treatment there is ample scope for genuine difference of opinion and one man clearly is not negligent merely because his conclusion differs from that of other professional men, nor because he has displayed less skill or knowledge than others would have shown. The true test for establishing negligence in diagnosis or treatment on the part of a doctor is whether he has been proved to be guilty of such failure as no doctor of ordinary skill would be guilty of if acting with ordinary care.

And in relation to the standard of such care when practice is alleged to have deviated from the ordinary or normal, the judge said:

> It follows from what I have said that in regard to allegations of deviation from ordinary professional practice . . . such a deviation is not necessarily evidence of negligence. Indeed it would be disastrous if this were so, for all inducement to progress in medical science would then be destroyed. Even a substantial deviation from normal practice may be warranted by the circumstances. To establish liability by a doctor where deviation from normal practice is alleged, three facts require to be established.
>
> First of all it must be proved that there is a usual and normal practice. Second by it must be proved that the defender [defendant] has not adopted that practice, and thirdly (and this is of

> crucial importance) it must be established that the course the doctor adopted is one which no professional man of ordinary skill would have taken if he had been acting with ordinary care.

The judge in the court below not having made this clear enough to the jury, a new trial was ordered in this case.

A limitation on the effect of the degree of discretion given to a practitioner on the basis of the decision in *Hunter v. Hanley* was, however, established in the case of *Clark v. MacLennan* (1983). The plaintiff, Mrs Clark, was about to give birth to her first child and was admitted to hospital for the confinement. Soon after the baby was delivered Mrs Clark began to suffer stress incontinence. This post-natal condition is not uncommon and involves loss of bladder control when mild physical stress has been experienced. Mrs Clark's own incontinence was particularly acute, and conventional treatment failed to improve her condition.

An anterior colporrhaphy operation was performed a month after the birth, but was unsuccessful. It is normal practice for gynaecologists not to perform this operation until at least three months after birth so as to ensure its success and to prevent the risk of haemorrhage. On this occasion haemorrhage did occur causing the repair to break down. Two further such operations were necessary, but neither was successful. As a result the stress incontinence suffered by the plaintiff became a permanent disability. She sued the gynaecologist and the health authority alleging negligence in the care and treatment given to her.

Mr Justice Peter Pain upheld her claim. He decided that, although in an action for negligence the burden of proof normally rests on the plaintiff, the present case was different. Where a general duty of care arises and there is a failure to take a recognised precaution, and that failure is followed by the very damage which the precaution is designed to prevent, the burden of proof lies on the defendant. The defendant must show, first, that he was not in breach of any duty and second, if he fails to prove he was not in breach of any duty, that the damage suffered by the plaintiff did not result from that breach.

A doctor owes a duty to his patient to take the precautions which are normal in the course of treatment he gives. The same principle applies to paramedical practitioners. Where a patient suffers damage following a departure from orthodox treatment, a court must inquire whether the practitioner took account of all proper factors, to determine whether that departure was in fact justified. Since in this case the doctor was not justified in his departure from normal practice, and since he failed to establish that the injury to the plaintiff had not been caused by this breach of duty, he was judged negligent.

Thus a case in which a normal precaution is not in fact taken, that precaution being one which is designed to avoid the very risk which materialises into injury to the plaintiff, can clearly be seen to differ both from a case in which there are two acceptable schools of thought, and also from a case in which, in relation to a single acceptable procedure, the practitioner has a discretion as to the most appropriate way to carry it out. Such a discretion does not exist where orthodoxy requires a specific precaution. It is for that reason that the burden of proving the acceptability of not taking the precaution, or of showing that the fact that it was not taken did not cause the injury, is placed upon the practitioner.

INJURY TO UNBORN CHILDREN

The cases discussed in this chapter have all concerned the normal instance of injury alleged to have been caused to people as independent human beings, that is, after their birth. There are, however, many instances in which injury may be negligently caused to a child before his birth. Examples include, for instance, therapy given in such a way that the unborn child receives injuries inside his mother, and injury from irradiation due to over-exposure (or even, if it could have been avoided, simple exposure) to harmful rays.

If a child is injured before birth the question arises as to whether he can, after birth, sue for damages in respect of injury received before he was born. In the case of *Williams v. Luff* (1978) a six-year-old boy was awarded damages in respect of injuries caused to him before his birth by the defendant motorist's negligent driving. Although the legal position of such a plaintiff to sue for ante-natal injuries was unclear, the defendant admitted liability, and the court was thus deprived of the opportunity to determine whether in law a duty of care is owed to an unborn child.

The position at common law is thus uncertain. By statute, however, unborn children do have certain rights in respect of protection against the consequences of negligent injuries to them. Under the Congenital Disabilities (Civil Liability) Act 1976, doubts as to the rights of the unborn child are removed in cases where the cause of the ante-natal injury can be proved; but liability to the child is also limited by the terms of the Act.

Under the Act an action may be brought on behalf of the child (or, later, by himself as an adult after attaining majority – see below) if the negligent defendant was answerable to the child in respect of one of two types of occurrence set out in section 1(2). An occurrence to which that section applies is: one which affected either parent of the child in his or her ability to have a normal, healthy child; or which affected the mother during her pregnancy, or affected her or the child in the course of birth, so that the child is born with disabilities which would not otherwise have been present. The child's right is thus a derivative right.

In the case of an ante-natal injury to the child it is not necessary for the mother to have been injured herself. It is suficient if there is a breach of a legal duty to her which would have given rise to liability in negligence had it caused injury to her. Nor is it even necessary that the defendant shall have known that the woman to whom he was in breach of a legal duty was in fact pregnant at the time of the occurrence. This results from the so-called 'eggshell skull' rule according to which a defendant takes his victim as he finds him or, in this case, her.

As to the time within which a congenitally disabled child must bring his action for damages, the rule is that proceedings must be commenced within three years of the child's reaching the age of majority. Practitioners are therefore faced with the somewhat daunting prospect of such an action being brought at any time within 21 years of the child's birth.

The standard of care expected of medical practitioners is specifically provided for in section 1(5) of the Act, and the same principle may be said to be applicable in the case of paramedical practitioners who might, through therapy or irradiation or other causes, be alleged to have been negligent in relation to the child's parent:

> The defendant is not answerable to the child, for anything he did or omitted to do when responsible in a professional capacity for treating or advising the parent, if he took reasonable care having due regard to then received professional opinion applicable to the particular class of case; but this does not mean he is answerable only because he departed from received opinion.

This section thus effectively enacts the common law principles of liability and responsibility of practitioners enunciated earlier in this chapter. That is, that acceptable practice precludes an action for negligence, and that even a departure from received opinion will not of itself establish liability. Whether or not it does so in fact will depend on the answers to the questions raised on *Clark v. MacLennan*, discussed above.

DUTY TO AVOID ECONOMIC LOSS

It may happen that a paramedical practitioner is sought to be made liable, not in respect of an act or statement causing physical harm to a patient, but on account of negligent advice given to the patient resulting in a lost or diminished compensation claim. If a practitioner is specifically consulted with a view to giving a professional opinion on, say, the extent and likely effect of certain physical injuries, a duty lies on that practitioner to avoid careless statements and careless diagnosis and prognosis which will foreseeably cause financial loss to the patient or client.

But the consultation must be conducted on the basis of a specific request for a professional opinion, and it is not enough to impose liability on the practitioner simply that the patient or client has a claim in mind. In a medical case, *Stevens v. Bermondsey and Southwark Group HMC* (1963), a casualty officer refused a patient's request for an *x*-ray and prescribed physiotherapy, saying nothing was seriously wrong. The patient settled a claim against a third party who had caused his injury for what he alleged was much less than he could have been awarded if the diagnosis had been careful and correct.

It was held, however, that in the absence of special circumstances surrounding the diagnosis, the doctor who made it was not required to contemplate or foresee any question connected with the third party's liability to his patient. Mr Justice Paull said that a doctor's duty is limited to the sphere of medicine and has nothing to do with the sphere of legal liability of a third party to his patient unless he examines with an eye to liability. Exactly the same principle will apply, with appropriate variations in the circumstances of the consultation, to paramedical practitioners.

PRESERVING TREATMENT RECORDS

An action in negligence may be commenced against a practitioner within three years of the occurrence of the personal injury alleged to have resulted from negligence, or within three years of the date on which the plaintiff first had knowledge that the injury was significant, that it was wholly or partly attributable to the alleged negligence, and knew the identity of the defendant. Even these time limits may be waived by the court in personal injury cases in which it appears equitable to do so. Actions for injuries to children may normally be brought within three years of majority. Actions for personal injuries brought by persons who were suffering from mental disorder may be brought within three years of their ceasing to be affected by the disorder.

It is therefore clear that practitioners are well advised to preserve records for at least a very long time after treatment. The absence of relevant records may be a great disadvantage in subsequent legal proceedings. Hospital and health service records are directed by circular HC(80)7 to be kept for a variety of minimum periods. In the case of children, for instance, personal health records should be kept at least until the patient's twenty-fifth birthday or until eight years after the last entry if longer. The periods stated are minimum periods, and the actual period may be longer according to guidelines given in the circular. Private practitioners might ask themselves whether it is ever advisable to destroy treatment records.

REFERENCES

[1] [1939] 2 K.B. 14, p. 31
[2] [1938] 4 All E.R. 85, p. 90
[3] [1957] 2 All E.R. 118, p. 122
[4] (1955) S.L.T. 213, p. 217

Chapter Eight

RESPONSIBILITY FOR PREMISES

The contents of this chapter have much in common with issues of care and standards of conduct which were raised in the previous chapter. When one person owes another a duty of care, and when a breach of that duty results in damage or injury, the result is actionable negligence. In the previous chapter we were mostly concerned with duties arising at common law, that is independently of the provisions of any statute.

In the present chapter too, attention focusses on duties and standards of care, this time in respect of the occupancy and control of premises. The legal duties of an occupier of premises owe their provenance partly to the common law. For instance, the modified duties of an occupier of premises towards trespassers are owed independently of the provisions of any statute. The principal source of the legal responsibilities of an occupier of premises, however, lies in statutory provisions, and in particular the Occupiers' Liability Act of 1957.

There are two quite distinct respects in which paramedical practitioners may be concerned with the safety of premises. First, and most frequently, they may be concerned with the safety of the premises on or in which practice is carried on. The question of responsibility will in such an instance relate to the legal liability of the paramedical practitioner towards patients or clients who come to the practice premises for treatment. As a very basic rule, the practice premises must be reasonably safe for the purposes for which the clients or patients attend.

A different aspect of the question of an occupier's responsibility for the safety of premises arises when the safety of paramedical practitioners themselves is concerned. Practitioners who work on health authority premises or on the premises of an employer such as a private hospital or the principals of a general medical practice will of course be interested in their own safety and well-being while at work on those premises. Their legitimate expectations were discussed in Chapters 5 and 6, when the legal responsibility of an employer or an employing authority towards employees was discussed.

The question was raised (p. 80) whether an employer might not also be legally responsible to an employee for the latter's well-being and safety while on a domiciliary visit to other premises, and the extent of such duty on an employer was examined. Such discussion does not, however, conclude the issue of legal liability for premises to which a domiciliary visit is made by a paramedical practitioner. For there remains the question of the responsibility which the law requires, for the practitioner's safety, of the person occupying the premises which are the subject of a domiciliary visit. The legal duties of an occupier of premises who receives a domiciliary visit will emerge in the course of this chapter as the responsibilities of an occupier towards all lawful visitors are examined.

WHO IS AN OCCUPIER?

The question of the legal responsibilities of an occupier of premises revolves not so much around the question of who occupies the premises in question, but rather around the question of who controls them. Normally, however, premises of the type likely to be used by paramedical practitioners for practice purpose will indeed be physically occupied by them; and premises on which they may work on behalf of an employer will be in the occupation of that employer. Occupational control may be shared between two or more people in respect of the same premises, as when practice premises are to some extent in common use between two or more people. Such, for instance, would be the case of practice premises in a building which contained shared hallways, staircases or toilet facilities. If an accident happened in that part of the premises which was shared, and breach of the legal duty shortly to be discussed could be proved, the person injured would be able to commence legal proceedings against each and every person sharing responsibility for the part of the premises on which the accident happened.

Lawful visitors

The legal responsibilities of an occupier in respect of premises safety are owed to all those whom the law now calls 'lawful visitors' to those premises. At one time a distinction used to be made by the law between 'invitees' and 'licensees'. This distinction did not coincide with the simple distinction between those who were specifically invited and those who were not so invited but were nevertheless lawfully on the premises (such as postmen). The distinction was, rather, between those people having some sort of common interest with the occupier of a financial or material kind (invitees) and those lawfully there but having no such common interest (licensees).

Since the Occupiers' Liability Act 1957, however, the law has not distinguished for liability purposes between these two classes of lawful entrant. Instead, the Act introduced a common concept. An occupier owes a common duty of care to all 'lawful visitors'. This term encompasses both the previous categories. Whether or not a person is in fact a lawful visitor meriting the kind of safeguards shortly to be discussed is a question which depends not only on the purpose of the visit but also upon the conduct of the visitor and the manifest intentions of the occupier.

The duty of care owed by an occupier to all lawful visitors does not extend to protect a visitor who goes into a part of the premises where no one would expect him to go. The case of a person straying from the permitted parts of the premises and becoming a trespasser is discussed below (p. 143). Furthermore, even a lawful visitor cannot expect the law's protection if he makes use of the permission to be there which is completely alien to the invitation. As Lord Justice Scrutton said in a case decided in 1927:[1] 'When you invite a person into your house to use the staircase you do not invite him to slide down the bannisters.'

As to the intentions of an occupier in relation to those who may claim to be owed a duty of care if they come on to the premises, clearly posted signs containing such messages as 'No hawkers' or 'No representatives without appointment' will turn such people into trespassers if they ignore them. Again, in such instances, the only duty of the occupier is the reduced obligation which may be owed to a trespasser.

The common duty of care

Section 2(2) of the Occupiers' Liability Act 1957 imposes upon an occupier of premises 'a duty to take such care as in all the circumstances of the case is reasonable to see that the visitor will be reasonably safe in using the premises for the purposes for which he is invited or permitted to be there'. This duty of care extends not only to the structure of the premises but also to fittings and fixtures, and to activities which are being carried on in the premises. So not only must steps, doorways, staircases and bannisters be reasonably safe for lawful visitors, but also carpets, furniture and equipment with which a patient or client is likely to come into contact or which could in some foreseeable way present a danger to such a person.

Whether or not the standard required by the common duty of care has been fulfilled by the occupier depends on the circumstances of each individual case. But the Act of 1957 does give some guidance in general terms as to what is expected of an occupier and what the occupier in turn may reasonably expect from those lawfully on the premises. Section 2(3) of the Act gives an indication of relevant circumstances which may affect the standard of care expected 'so that (for example) in proper cases: (a) an occupier must be prepared for children to be less careful than adults; and (b) an occupier may expect that a person, in the exercise of his calling, will appreciate and guard against any risks ordinarily incident to it, so far as the occupier leaves him free to do so.'

Example (a) is self-explanatory and an occupier must always be mindful of the standard of precautions appropriate to children who are lawfully on the premises. Example (b) applies not to the ordinary case of a client or patient but to a person who comes on to the premises, for instance, to carry out maintenance or repair work. In the case of *Bates v. Parker* (1953) Lord Goddard said [2] that 'where a householder employs an independent contractor (p. 52) to do work, be it of cleaning or repairing, on his premises, the contractor must satisfy himself as to the safety or condition of that part of the premises on which he is to work.'

The question arises as to whether a paramedical practitioner engaged on a domiciliary visit to a patient's own premises may fall to be considered in relation to example (b). In the normal course of events the practitioner will not fall within these considerations, for the reasonable safety of the premises and of furniture, fittings and equipment on them will have no connection with the special purpose for which the visit is made. So a faulty light switch or a dangerous stair carpet will be just as much a danger to a practitioner engaged on a domiciliary visit to the premises as they would be to anyone else and are just as likely to entitle the visiting practitioner to damages in the event of injury.

It might, however, happen that an examination table or equipment which had been installed for the purpose of therapy was in a dangerous condition. If the practitioner or the practitioner's employer or employing authority was responsible for the special use of the premises in this particular aspect, the occupier would be entitled to rely on the practitioner's appreciation of any special risks presented by the fittings or equipment in question. The practitioner would, in the words of the Act, be reasonably expected to 'guard against any special risks ordinarily incident to it.'

Where the situation involves the practitioner as an occupier, as it does in the case of patients and clients coming for treatment at the practice premises, the general rule applies that a duty is owed to such people to take such care as is reasonable to see that they are reasonably safe in using the premises for the purpose for which they come there. If, therefore, there is some special equipment or furniture which could reasonably be expected to present a danger if not, for instance, adequately maintained, the duty of the practitioner-occupier will extend to such equipment in the same way that it applies to non-specialist items such as the furnishings and carpeting.

A further consideration relevant to the visit of patients and clients to therapists is the fact that some, perhaps many of them, may be in some way disabled, albeit temporarily. They may be suffering from a condition which makes them less able to take proper care for their own well-being and safety. If the practitioner whose premises are visited for purposes of consultation knows or should know about the perils in which a particular client may be placed, a correspondingly higher duty is owed to that person.

Though the 'common duty of care' is by definition common to all lawful visitors, including all patients and clients, the particular precautions appropriate to an individual case will vary. As a general rule both of law and of good sense, the greater the disability of, or peril to, a particular patient of which the practitioner-occupier knows or ought to know, the greater will be the duty of care owed to that person in respect of safety on practice premises.

For instance, the entrance door to the practice premises might be fitted with a spring to make it close automatically behind entrants on their arrival. The practitioner who occupies the premises is clearly under a duty to see that the spring is not so strong that an infirm or disabled patient might foreseeably be injured by the way in which the door is fitted.

Clients and patients are of course expected to show adequate concern for their own safety and well-being on the practice premises. Therefore although elderly or infirm visitors may be owed a higher degree of care than normal, they are not expected to behave in such a foolhardy manner that they positively invite injury. The duty of the practitioner-occupier is certainly not so high that every slip amounts to the breach of a legal duty to the client. The general statement of the duty of care in the 1957 Act may again be recalled. It requires an occupier to exercise such care as in all the circumstances of the case is reasonable to see that the visitor will be reasonably safe in using the premises for the purpose for which he or she is there.

The practitioner-occupier clearly exercises an extensive degree of control over the way in which premises are used, and as to the parts of those premises into which visitors may go, be they patients or clients or anyone else who is lawfully there (say a client's relative or children). There are two aspects of this control which require specific consideration. One is that an occupier of premises may well wish to give warning of a danger either verbally or by a notice in or outside the premises. The other is that an occupier of practice premises may wish to go beyond a mere warning of danger (such as 'Mind the step') and actually disclaim legal liability for any injury caused to a visitor. The matter of warnings is examined first. After that the question of disclaimers will be examined in respect of the differing considerations applicable to patients visiting practice premises and practitioners paying domiciliary visits to patients.

Warnings

The Occupiers' Liability Act 1957 envisages the giving of warnings by an occupier and has this to say in section 2(4)(a):

> Where damage is caused to a visitor by a danger of which he had been warned by the occupier, the warning is not to be treated without more as absolving the occupier from liability, unless in all the circumstances it was enough to enable the visitor to be reasonably safe.

There may be two separate types of circumstance in which the warning is not in fact adequate to discharge the common duty of care owed by an occupier to lawful visitors. First, the wording of the notice itself may be inadequate to explain the danger. This possibility of an intrinsic inadequacy in a would-be warning notice is obvious and requires no further comment. But a second circumstance in which a would-be warning of danger is in fact inadequate to discharge the occupier's legal duty relates not to the notice itself but to those to whom it is sought to apply.

Again, considerations of the particular inadequacies or disabilities of patients and clients come into question. For instance, it would be manifestly unreasonable, and so no discharge of the requisite legal duty, to put a warning sign so high that infirm patients who are normally looking downward are unable to see it by any reasonable means. Warning signs may, on the other hand, be perfectly adequate to discharge the requisite legal duty of an occupier in the great majority of cases but not in an exceptional case.

For instance, a reasonably-placed and clearly-worded warning of danger might be most adequate for sighted people. But if a practitioner knows or has reason to know that a particular client is blind or partially-sighted, a warning adequate to others would not be sufficient in such a case. Similar considerations apply also in the case of attempts by an occupier of premises to disclaim legal liability for injury occasioned on those premises to lawful visitors.

Disclaimers and exclusion of liability

The question of excluding legal liability in the case of injuries to lawful visitors has some features in common with that of giving warnings. For instance, in considering the adequacy of either for the purpose for which it is designed by the occupier, regard should be had not just to lawful visitors in general but also to specific infirmities or disabilities of particular patients of which the practitioner-occupier knows or ought to know.

But in other respects the questions of warning and exclusion of liability are distinct and independent. If an occupier gives warning of a danger, this is an attempt to discharge the common duty of care which the occupier owes to lawful visitors. If, on the other hand, the occupier posts on the premises an exclusion or disclaimer notice the intention behind it is very different. For such a notice does nothing towards discharging the requisite duty of care to those on the premises. What it does is to state the intentions of the occupier to lawful visitors in respect of his legal liability, or rather the absence of such liability, towards them.

A different case still is the position of a trespasser on the practice premises or in the grounds. The obviously limited obligations of an occupier towards trespassers are considered below. They are mentioned at this point simply in order to exclude them from the matter immediately in issue. A warning or notice making it clear to trespassers that their presence is not wanted, seeks to exclude them from the premises, or from a particular part of the premises, altogether. An exclusion clause, by contrast, demonstrates not an intention to keep people out, but rather an intention to disclaim liability to them once they are lawfully in.

The question therefore arises as to whether, and if so under what conditions, an occupier of premises is lawfully able to exclude liability in respect of loss, injury or damage suffered by someone lawfully on the premises. Section 2(1) of the Occupiers' Liability Act 1957 states that an occupier owes the common duty of care to all lawful visitors 'except in so far as he is free to and does extend, restrict, modify or exclude his duty to any visitor or visitors by agreement or otherwise'. The Act therefore clearly envisages circumstances in which an occupier's liability for injury to visitors may lawfully be excluded. In order to demonstrate the extent to which such exclusion of liability may be lawfully permitted, the facts of a case decided shortly before the 1957 Act will be considered, and following that the provisions of a 1977 statute which set important limits to the conditions in which liability may lawfully be excluded.

The case of *Ashdown v. Samuel Williams & Sons* (1957) demonstrates the position of exclusion notices at common law, that is independently of statutory provisions which may prevail over the common law position. The provision of the 1957 Act cited above causes reference to be made to both the common law position and to any statute which may limit or alter that position.

The plaintiff in this case was lawfully on land belonging to and occupied by the defendant company. She was knocked down and injured as a result of the negligent shunting of some railway trucks on a private line on the land. The company had put up various notices to the effect that people on the land were there at their own risk and would have no claim against the company for any injury whatsoever. The court decided in favour of the defendant company, stating that they had in fact taken reasonable steps to bring the conditions contained in the exclusion notices to the plaintiff's attention.

Though subsequently subjected to criticism, this decision represents the common law in respect of the extent to which an occupier is, under Section 2(1) of the Occupiers' Liability Act 1957, lawfully permitted to exclude his duty of care to visitors. It is a rule of law, therefore, that such an exclusion or disclaimer may be permissible. Whether or not the notice is adequate in all the circumstances of the particular case to exclude liability is a question of fact.

Given that liability to lawful visitors may be excluded at common law, it is necessary to consider the effect on that common law position made by the Unfair Contract Terms Act 1977. The Occupiers' Liability Act provides that an occupier may exclude liability if free to do so. The Unfair Contract Terms Act sets out conditions in which certain occupiers are not free to do so. 'Certain' occupiers is said advisedly, for the restrictions on exclusion clauses set out in the 1977 Act relate only to things done in the course of a business or from the occupation of premises used for business purposes of the occupier (s. 1(3)).

A distinction therefore has to be drawn between exclusion of liability for injuries on premises not used for business purposes, as in the normal case of premises to which a domiciliary visit is made; and attempts to exclude injury liability in respect of premises used for the business of the practice. In the case of a patient's premises to which a domiciliary visit is made there is in reality little if any likelihood of the patient-occupier seeking to exclude injury liability in respect of lawful visitors, including paramedical practitioners. But if such an attempt were made, the law could recognise it as valid. The only question would be whether in fact the conditions upon which the practitioner and other lawful visitors were permitted to enter the premises had been brought reasonably to their attention.

In the case, however, of practice premises falling within the definition of 'premises used for business purposes of the occupier,' Section 2 of the Unfair Contract Terms Act 1977 invalidates even the attempt to exclude liability for personal injury and death on the premises, thus making it irrelevant whether or not the lawful visitor saw the notice or could reasonably have been expected to see it. Section 2 of the Act provides that a person cannot by reference to any contract term or to a notice exclude or restrict his liability for death or personal injury resulting from negligence.

The 'notice' mentioned in this prohibition against exclusion of negligence liability refers to the sort of sign on or at the edge of premises such as was relied on successfully in the case of *Ashdown v. Samuel Williams & Sons*, above. It is worth noting that the actual circumstances in that case would, since the 1977 Act, lead to the opposite conclusion to that which was reached. This is because the premises on which the plaintiff was injured by the negligent shunting operations were being used for purposes of the occupier's business. The case nevertheless remains authority for the proposition that a non-business occupier may still exclude injury liability.

As will be explained below, however, the law now requires some kind of care to be taken even in certain cases of trespass on premises. The so-called 'duty of ordinary humanity', which may be owed to trespassers, is probably not capable of exclusion by an occupier in relation to lawful visitors. Otherwise trespassers would be in a better position than lawful visitors subject to an exclusion notice.

A non-business occupier remains equally free from legal restriction against exclusions relating to property damage occurring on the premises as well as in respect of personal injury, save that in both cases the policy of the law is to give a narrow interpretation to any such exclusion. An occupier using premises for business, including practice, purposes is permitted in principle to exclude or modify liability in respect of damage to patients' property. But here again the Unfair Contract Terms Act of 1977 introduced a restriction on the extent to which such exclusions are valid.

Section 2 of the 1977 Act further provides that, in the case of damage other than physical injury, a person using premises for business purposes cannot exclude or restrict his liability for negligence except in so far as the term or notice satisfies the requirement of reasonableness. What is in fact reasonable in a particular case will depend both on the way in which the exclusion notice is framed and on the circumstances in which it is claimed to operate against the lawful visitor, in this context the client or patient.

No general rule can be laid down in advance since each case will differ in its circumstances from the next. It may be surmised, however, by way of example, that a notice purporting to exclude the practitioner-occupier's liability for damage to patients' property when such property was instructed to be left in a dangerous or ramshackle part of the premises, would not be regarded as a reasonable and therefore valid exclusion.

The case of loss of property, both that of patients when visiting practice premises and also that of the practitioner's own property taken to a patient's premises on a domiciliary visit, stands on a different footing from the question of damage, and is now examined in general terms applicable to both contexts.

Loss of property

While the Occupiers' Liability Act 1957 maintains in operation the previous common law rules relating to damage to lawful visitors' property, it does nothing to affect the further common law rule in respect of loss of property. That rule, which continues to represent the law, is that an occupier of premises has no duty to protect visitors' property against the risk of theft by third parties. The case of damage to such property has already been discussed in the context of exclusion notices. The basis of discussion was that, in the absence of such a disclaimer, the occupier would be liable for damage caused to visitors' property as the result of the occupier's breach of the common duty of care.

But loss of visitors' property caused by the unlawful intervention of a third party, for instance a thief, stands on a different footing. The relevant rule is illustrated by a case which in fact occurred on premises occupied by a health authority and which is therefore of additional practical relevance to paramedical practitioners and trainees who live in premises rented from a health authority.

In *Edwards v. West Herts Group HMC* (1957) the plaintiff was employed as a house physician at a hospital. His terms of employment stated that he had to live at a staff hostel adjoining the hospital and that a portion of his salary would be deducted for board and lodging. A number of his belongings were stolen from his room, and he brought an action against the health authority alleging that, through its officers, it had failed to take reasonable care of his room and the effects which it contained.

The county court judge dismissed the doctor's action, and he appealed against this decision to the Court of Appeal. That court held that the relationship between the parties was not that of a boarding-house keeper and boarder (in which a duty of care would have been owed), but that of employer and employee. An employer, said the Court of Appeal, is under no duty to take reasonable care to prevent the theft of his employee's effects.

Lord Justice Hodson further explained in his judgement that the rule in respect of the non-liability for loss of property extends beyond the employer-employee situation and is of general application, save in respect of the special contractual relationship existing between keepers of boarding-houses and guest-houses and their visitors. He cited the judgement of Lord Justice Jenkins in *Tinsley v. Dudley* (1951) to this effect:

> There is no warrant at all on the authorities, so far as I know, for holding that an invitor [p. 134] where the invitation extends to the goods as well as the person of the invitee, thereby by implication of law assumes a liability to protect the invitee and

his goods, not merely from physical dangers arising from defects in the premises, but from the risk of the goods being stolen by some third party. That implied liability, so far as I know, is one unknown to the law.[3]

LIABILITY TO TRESPASSERS

The discussion in this chapter has so far proceeded on the basis that the person 'visiting' the premises in question was lawfully there. It now remains to consider the legal relationship between an occupier of premises and someone who is unlawfully on the premises, or on a particular part of the premises in respect of which express or implied permission to enter is lacking. The relationship to be considered is therefore that between an occupier and a trespasser.

It might seem odd at first glance that a trespasser should have any rights at all against an occupier of premises. On reflection, however, it is not at all surprising that there should be a common law rule that an occupier may not lawfully do anything to cause deliberate or reckless injury to a trespasser. Protection of property by alarms, and even by spiked railings provided they are reasonably in evidence, is perfectly permissible. But the setting of traps to injure intruders is not. The Occupiers' Liability Act 1957 did nothing to affect this common law position.

It would, on the other hand, be even more odd if an occupier of premises owed a complete duty to trespassers in respect of their safety while trespassing on the premises, and indeed the common duty of care as laid down in the 1957 Act has no application to trespassers. Nevertheless a decision of the House of Lords in 1972 is authority for the proposition that an occupier may in certain circumstances owe a duty to a trespasser which is higher than the mere duty to refrain from causing the trespasser deliberate or reckless injury.

In the case of *British Railways Board v. Herrington* (1972) a small boy was severely injured by electrocution as a result of straying from a field through a gap in a poorly-maintained fence and on to an electric railway line. The local station master had been informed about the gap in the fence bordering the railway line and that children had been seen on the line. The only action he took, however, was to inform the police. Although it was argued on behalf of the defendants that there had been no breach of duty on the part of the Railways Board, through its employees, the House of Lords decided the case in favour of the injured child plaintiff.

In so deciding their Lordships laid down a type of intermediate duty to trespassers, more demanding than the mere duty to refrain from deliberate or reckless injury but stopping necessarily short of the duty owed by an occupier to lawful visitors. This duty is frequently described as a duty to act with ordinary or common humanity in the face of clear risks to the trespasser concerned. It may apply to adults as well as to children.

An occupier is under no legal obligation to take steps to investigate the premises for the presence of trespassers, nor to carry out positive checks to ensure that no dangers exist which may cause injury to trespassers. But, since the *Herrington* case, a limited duty may be placed upon the occupier if there has been something to bring the presence of trespassers to the occupier's attention, or if he actually knows of facts which make it likely that trespassers will come on to the premises. The duty to trespassers is also dependent on actual knowledge on the part of the occupier about conditions on his premises which are likely to cause personal injury to a trespasser who is unaware of the danger.

The duty to trespassers is, in contradistinction to the relatively predictable common duty of care laid down in the 1957 Act, highly specific to the facts of each individual case. It is not a duty to make the premises safe for trespassers, but rather the more limited duty to take steps which will enable the 'likely' trespasser to avoid the danger. Once the occupier has actual knowledge of the likelihood of trespassers and of the likelihood of their being injured by a danger of which they are unaware, the court will examine all the circumstances of the particular case in order to determine whether the occupier has fallen below the duty of ordinary humanity.

Lord Diplock set out the factors which will be material to the court's determination of such a question:

> The degree of likelihood needed to give rise to the duty cannot, I think, be more closely defined than as being such as would impel a man of ordinary humane feelings to take some steps to mitigate the risk of injury to the trespasser to which the particular danger exposes him. It will thus depend on all the circumstances of the case: the permanent or intermittent character of the danger; the severity of the injuries which it is likely to cause; in the case of children, the attractiveness to them of that which constitutes the dangerous object or condition of the land; the expense involved in giving effective warning of it to the kind of

trespasser likely to be injured, in relation to the occupier's resources in money or in labour.[4]

It should be added, finally, that the category of trespasser includes not only those whose initial entry on to the premises is unlawful but also those whose initial presence was lawful but whose presence becomes unpermitted and therefore unlawful by, for instance, going through a door clearly marked 'Private' or 'No Admittance'. Whether or not the occupier will be able to rely on such a notice and consequently treat the person concerned as unlawfully on a particular part of the premises so marked, will depend upon the considerations as to the adequacy and reasonableness of the particular notice which were discussed above in relation to signs and notices warning of a danger on the premises. A practitioner will not, for instance, be entitled to rely on a notice purporting to restrict the parts of the practice premises on which the presence of others is lawfully permitted if the particular person against whom the notice is sought to be used did not have a reasonable opportunity to read it or understand it.

REFERENCES

[1] *The Calgarth* [1927] p. 93. p. 110
[2] [1953] 2 Q.B. 231, p. 235
[3] [1951] 1 W.L.R. 415, p. 417
[4] [1972] 1 All E.R. 749, p. 796

Chapter Nine

CONSENT AND CONFIDENTIALITY

This chapter examines two important obligations owed by practitioners to their clients: the obligation to obtain a patient's consent to treatment, and the duty to maintain a patient's confidences. In the case of both, a relatively greater emphasis is placed upon the legitimate expectations of patients and clients.

A common feature of these obligations is that they are both to some extent conditioned by patient choice. It might at first sight be tempting to describe the rights of patients to agree to what is to be done to them and to what is to be said about them as rights of 'self-determination'. To describe the obligations in this way would, however, be to indicate that both are fundamentally rooted in a choice exercisable by the patient or client. And this would be to over-generalise the principles of confidentiality, and would positively misrepresent the legal rules relating to consent to treatment.

In the case of the duty to maintain confidentiality a number of exceptions can be made to the general rule of secrecy, even though the obligation itself is rooted in the patient's choice about disclosure and non-disclosure.

In the case of consent to treatment, the present legal position in England is even further from an overal principle of self-determination. Whereas consent is a notion signifying agreement and free choice, the courts of this country have not so far based the duty to obtain a patient's consent to treatment squarely on the patient's own choice.

The lawfulness and the propriety of what is to be done by way of treatment and what is to be relayed by way of information requires attention to the patient's own choice. But, in both instances, the way in which the law recognises this element of choice is a long way from being dictated by the patient.

TREATMENT AND CONSENT

The general rule is that any direct physical contact with another person without that person's consent amounts in law to a battery. It gives grounds for an action for damages without the need to prove that any actual harm or injury has been sustained. A beneficent motive will not render lawful a physical contact or interference with another's person which is done without consent. It may, however, significantly affect the damages awarded in respect of a technically wrongful act if the recipient of treatment without consent has thereby been saved from death or from serious damage to health.

The general rule that physical contact, including treatment, without consent is unlawful is subject to necessary exceptions in the case of those who are for some reason unable to give or to refuse consent to proposed treatment. Such is most obviously the case with patients who are unconscious, say when brought into the casualty department for attention. Others who are incapable of giving or refusing consent are young children and those who are so mentally disordered that they cannot understand what is involved. Treatment of the unconscious, the young and the mentally disordered is discussed later.

Battery, like assault, is a variety of the tort (or wrong) of trespass to the person. An assault is an act which causes in the person subjected to it an apprehension of the immediate infliction of a battery. A battery is the physical contact itself with another's person. Approaching a non-consenting patient with a hypodermic syringe amounts, if the patient apprehends the imminent physical contact, to an assault. The actual giving of the injection in the absence of consent is a battery. Frequently the two varieties of trespass will be combined in the same situation. But battery alone may be committed, say in the case of an unconscious patient who cannot experience the apprehension required for assault.

As is the case with all forms of trespass, assault and battery are actionable without the need to prove actual harm or injury. These legal wrongs therefore make a substantial contribution to the protection of a person's civil liberties, or at any rate to compensation for wrongful interference with them. If, however, there is consent to the physical contact or to the treatment or procedure in question, trespass to the person is not committed. The patient may still have an action if the treatment or procedure for which consent was given is carried out in a careless way and harm or injury ensues. The question will then be decided according to the rules and principles of negligence liability discussed in Chapter 7.

Certain distinctions should at once be noted as between assault and battery on the one hand, and negligence on the other. As was explained in Chapter 7 the requirement of damage, in the sense of harm or injury, is of the very essence of a negligence action. Furthermore, the elements of duty of care and breach of that duty as a result of the defendant's falling below the requisite standard of care which a negligence action requires, are irrelevant to an action for assault or battery. In the case of these wrongs, the only duty involved is a duty to refrain from committing them. But the law does not require proof of the breach of this 'duty' as a separate element. It is enough if the wrong is simply committed; the general 'duty' not to commit wrongs goes without saying.

The distinctions between trespass (assault and battery) and negligence assume a particular importance when it comes to examining precisely what it is which a patient should consent to. Must consent, if an action for trespass to the person is to be avoided, be given merely in respect of physical contact as such? Or must it be given in respect of the general nature and purpose of the treatment in question? Or must it, still more specifically, be given in respect of particular risks which may be involved? These questions point to the problems of informed consent to treatment which is discussed later (p. 150).

Express and implied consent

The general legal requirement of consent to treatment may be evidenced by what the patient says or writes, or it may be inferred from the patient's conduct. Express consent, in either oral or written form, is the more reliable way of obtaining the agreement requisiste to the avoidance of an action for trespass to the person. In the case of surgical operations it is normal practice to obtain a patient's written consent to treatment, and the usual way of effecting this is to use standard forms of operation consent.

Consent given by word of mouth is just as valid in law as consent in writing. The difference between the two ways of obtaining consent lies in their practical rather than their legal consequences. If a patient later complained that he had not in fact agreed to a particular treatment or procedure, his signature on a form indicating that the nature of the procedure in question had been explained to him and that he agreed to undergo it would constitute very strong evidence of consent which the patient would find very difficult to disprove.

In the case of treatments and procedures less than surgical operations, however, consent will normally be given orally or even simply inferred from conduct. It is therefore with these two ways of obtaining a patient's consent that paramedical practitioners are likely to be concerned in the great majority of cases. If a procedure is being performed on a patient for the first time it will usually be advisable to explain to the patient or client the nature and the purpose of what is proposed. Such an explanation will normally be brief and it will usefully be couched in sufficiently non-technical language to enable the patient properly to understand.

When procedures are repeated on a second or further occasion it will normally be reasonable to rely on the patient's conduct in submitting to what is clearly about to be done. A repeated explanation of exactly the same procedures will usually be laborious and redundant. If, on the other hand, the procedure is ostensibly the same but there is in fact a significant variation in its intended effect, express consent is advisable. For example, a further diathermy treatment or a further irradiation of a patient may significantly increase the heat or the dosage respectively which the patient is intended to receive, even if to all outward appearances the procedure looks the same to the patient.

If a second or further treatment were to be given on the basis of an increase in heat, radiation or other relevant dosage without an explanation to the patient of this increase, the question arises as to whether any, and if so what, legal wrong would be committed by the practitioner. Judging by the principles so far discussed in relation to treatment given without a patient's consent, it might be expected that an action for battery would succeed against the defendant practitioner.

The courts in this country have, however, shown themselves to be unwilling to rely on the law relating to trespass to the person in cases in which resort may alternatively be had to the tort of negligence. The instance just mentioned contains aspects which might attract the application of either battery or negligence.

In favour of battery it could be said that while earlier treatments had been fully consented to, the increased dosage amounts to a substantially different treatment. Since this new treatment was unexplained, it was therefore given without consent and amounted to battery. In favour of negligence, on the other hand, it would be argued that the patient was aware of the general nature of the treatment and that the increased dosage or measure altered the treatment in degree only and not in kind.

It appears that much the more likely judicial attitude would be to regard a case such as this not as battery but as negligence. In that event, unlike an action for battery, the patient would have to prove not only a breach of duty on the part of the practitioner but also harm or injury resulting from that breach. If no damage resulted, an action for negligence would fail.

If damage did result from this increased dosage or measure given without consent it would have to be asked whether this damage resulted from negligent treatment (the principles of which were examined in Chapter 7), or rather from the materialisation of a risk inherent in treatment which itself had been carried out with reasonable care. The question of information about inherent risks, over and above information about the nature of the proposed treatment, involves the problem of informed consent, which is now examined.

Informed consent to treatment

If a patient is informed of the nature and purpose of the treatment or procedure which is proposed, then any consent obtained as a result will be a good defence against an action for battery. If, of course, the practitioner's explanation was given in bad faith with the deliberate intention of misleading the patient, the apparent consent will in fact be unreal and invalid. In that case an action for battery would be available just as readily as if no explanation at all had been given.

It is possible to argue that not only the nature and purpose of the proposed treatment but also the inherent risks contained in it should be explained if true consent is to be given by the patient; and, further, that a failure to explain such risks invalidates any apparent consent given by the patient, thus entitling him to sue the practitioner concerned for battery. The argument runs that the inherent risks are themselves an integral part of the proposed treatment, and that the general nature and the risks stand on the same footing. As will be seen, however, English law prefers to regard a failure to explain risks as negligence and not as grounds for an action for battery.

It was suggested in the introduction to this chapter that the legitimate expectations of patients to receive an explanation of proposed treatment are rooted in their rights of self-determination. When it comes to reflecting patient expectation in its rules relating to consent to treatment, a legal system is faced with a choice. This choice is whether to place the greater emphasis on the right of the patient to receive information or on the duty of practitioners to give it, basing that duty at least in part on the practitioner's professional judgement.

If the procedure or treatment is truly elective, as it will be in cases other than those in which there is a substantial imbalance between slight risks in treatment and risk of grave harm to health if it is not given, the patient's own choice would seem to be paramount. The law might then be expected to make the requirement of an explanation of risks depend on what the particular patient would want explained. It would look to the sort of explanation a particular patient would need in order to come to a rational decision whether or not to proceed with the proposed treatment. Or at least, if that requirement were to appear altogether too subjective, then at least what a reasonable or prudent patient would require in order to make such a decision.

That this is not the legal position in England is shown by a number of judicial decisions which make it clear that the adequacy of explanation is assessed not on the basis of patient expectation but rather according to the professional judgement of the practitioner. The principles in question have been evolved in cases concerning medical practitioners but are equally applicable to explanations given by paramedical practitioners to their patients or clients.

In this way, the cases show, the right of the patient to receive information becomes translated into a part of the general duty of care which the practitioner owes to a patient. Put another way, the question of what risks to disclose and which ones to withhold is subsumed under the more general duty to exercise professional or clinical judgement with reasonable care.

There is no duty to inform a patient that treatment might be performed without reasonable care. If such a 'risk' were to materialise and the patient were to be injured in consequence, a straightforward action in negligence would be brought.

Compared with cases involving allegations of negligence in treatment, relatively few decisions are available in England as to the risks which a practitioner needs to disclose to a patient if he is to discharge his duty of care and avoid an allegation of negligence. In keeping with the patient's own self-determination the natural question to ask would relate to which of the risks inherent in treatment the patient would expect to be disclosed. The patient could then be said to be exercising self-determination in the choice whether or not to submit to the proposed procedure or treatment.

The reality of the matter in English law is very different. Until recently the question which the courts asked themselves was not the question as to which of the risks inherent in proposed treatment should be disclosed, but rather whether any risks at all should be disclosed to the patient. In posing this very basic question the courts have approached the problem broadly in relation to two different types of case. The first is that in which the patient actually asks about risks involved in treatment. The second concerns statements volunteered to patients without any question having been asked. The required explanation does not, however, differ substantially between the two types of case.

The inquiring patient

In *Hatcher v. Black* (1954) the plaintiff was a singer who broadcast occasionally for the BBC. She went into hospital suffering from a toxic thyroid gland and was advised to have an operation. She might have been given drug therapy. But such treatment would have extended over a long period, and she was encouraged to have a partial thyroidectomy instead. During the operation the laryngeal nerve was badly damaged, so much so that she could not speak properly and could not broadcast again. The plaintiff's action against the surgeon for negligent performance of the operation failed.

The case is relevant to the present context, however, in that the patient not surprisingly asked her physician whether or not the recommended surgical procedure would involve any risk to her voice. In reply, she alleged, her physician advised her that there was no risk whatever involved. Lord Justice Denning (as he was then) directed the jury to consider whether they believed as a fact that the physician had told the plaintiff this untruth, and, if so, whether they thought him open to censure for doing so. Incidentally, juries are no longer used in civil actions of this kind. Such a case is now tried by a judge alone, dealing with both law and fact.

The surgeon who performed the operation admitted in his evidence that he too had told the patient, the night before the operation, that no risk was involved. He knew there was, but did so in order that she would not worry. In relation to the surgeon (it was not he who was sued for allegedly misleading the plaintiff, but the physician), Lord Justice Denning said:

> What should the doctor tell his patient? Mr Tuckwell [the surgeon] admitted that on the evening of the operation he told the plaintiff that there was no risk to her voice, when he knew that there was some slight risk, but that he did it for her own good because it was of vital importance that she should not worry. In short, he told a lie, but he did it because he thought in the circumstances it was justifiable. If this were a court of morals, that would raise a nice question on which moralists and theologians have differed for centuries. Some hold that it is never permissible to tell a lie even for a just cause: a good end, they say, does not justify a bad means. You must not do a little wrong in order to do a great right.
>
> Others, however, hold that it is permissible, if the justification is strong enough and they point to the stratagems used in war to deceive the enemy. This, however, is not a court of morals but a court of law, and the law leaves this question of morals to the conscience of the doctor himself – though I may perhaps remark that if doctors have too easy a conscience on this matter they may in time lose the confidence of their patient, which is the basis of good medicine.
>
> But so far as the law is concerned, it does not condemn the doctor when he only does that which many a wise and good doctor so placed would do. It only condemns him when he falls short of the accepted standards of a great profession; in short, when he is deserving of censure. No one of the doctors that have been called before you has suggested that Mr Tuckwell did wrong. All agree that it was a matter for his own judgement. They did not condemn him; nor should we.

And the jury did not, indeed, condemn him but found in favour of both the defendants, physician and surgeon alike. The result of this decision is that a patient's freedom of choice even in a truly elective medical or surgical procedure is considerably limited. Not only did the jury's verdict, strongly indicated by Lord Justice Denning's guidance to them, tacitly approve the withholding of information about alternative drug therapy, upon which the patient would have been able to make a more rational and informed choice. But also, a positive untruth about the risks inherent in the one treatment which was offered was allowed to pass.

Further evidence of the same judicial approach is found in the New Zealand Court of Appeal decision in *Smith v. Auckland Hospital Board* (1964). Although the court in fact decided the case in the plaintiff patient's favour the judgement contained statements envisaging a wide discretion in respect of permissible answers to patient inquiries. The plaintiff entered hospital for an examination and, if necessary, surgical treatment for a suspected aortic aneurysm. During proper preliminary investigations he underwent aortography whereby a catheter was inserted into the femoral artery and guided towards the aorta. Opaque fluid was then injected to enable the aorta to be outlined for radiographic purposes. The procedure went wrong, clotting occurred in the artery, causing gangrene, and the patient's leg had to be amputated.

The plaintiff had asked the doctor carrying out the aortogram 'Is there any risk attached to this?' In his evidence the doctor said he could not remember the exact words he used in his reply. But the patient maintained that the reply he received was: 'Old chap, within a couple of days you will be back home. You will be under a light anaesthetic and you will know nothing about it.' The doctor accepted that nothing was said about there being any risk.

The decision of the New Zealand Court of Appeal in favour of the plaintiff patient is authority for the following proposition. The relationship of doctor and patient is sufficient to impose upon the doctor a duty to use due care in answering a question put to him by the patient where the patient, to the knowledge of the doctor, intends to place reliance on that answer in making a decision as to a treatment or procedure to which he is asked to consent.

If, in answering such a question, a doctor fails to use due care, and the patient is injured as a result of submitting to the treatment, the doctor is liable to the patient if the evidence shows that it is probable that if a proper answer had been given, the patient would have refused to undergo the treatment either immediately or after further questions and answers.

In finding for the plaintiff, however, the court was at pains to emphasise that it was not seeking to lay down any general rule as to requisite replies to patient questions, still less as to what should be volunteered where no questions are asked. The doctor's reply to the patient's question overstepped the permissible bounds of medical discretion. A proper answer, said the court, will vary with the circumstances of each case, and what is proper will require expert medical evidence as to what is generally accepted practice. Chief Justice Barrowclough stated in his judgement:

> . . . it cannot always be said – especially when a patient is asking questions of his doctor – that the doctor is bound to give a full, complete and true answer. Much may depend on the effect of the answer on the health of the patient.

If, therefore, the doctor decides to answer the patient's question, the decision in *Smith v. Auckland Hospital Board* clearly shows that the doctor is under a duty to exercise care in answering it. But that duty of care is heavily influenced by expert medical evidence as to generally accepted practice. Furthermore, given that generally accepted medical practice may countenance untruths if they are considered to be 'therapeutic', the restrictions on the patient's opportunities for self-determination are clear and considerable.

Application of these decisions

When a doctor deliberately misinforms a patient 'for his own good' about risks which the doctor knows are inherent in the proposed treatment, the assumption is that the patient is motivated purely by medical considerations. That assumption is borne out by the overriding factor, accepted by judge and jury alike, that information may justifiably be withheld in order to prevent the patient's condition and the success of the proposed treatment being adversely affected by worry. In fact patients may well be motivated not only by medical considerations in their decision whether or not to proceed with proposed treatment, but also by social, financial, emotional and various other non-medical reasons.

While the discussion of paramedical liability in Chapter 7 proceeded upon the basis that the rules and principles applicable in cases involving medical practitioners are equally applicable in the case of their paramedical counterparts, a note of caution should be introduced into the present examination of adequate explanations in obtaining consent to treatment. The decisions in these two cases clearly give medical practitioners a wide discretion not only about what to disclose and what not to disclose, but also as to the factual accuracy of that which is disclosed.

For the purpose of considering whether the same discretion might be available in the case of paramedical practitioners involved in patient treatment, a distinction might be drawn between those engaged in private practice to whom patients or clients come directly without referral by a medical practitioner, and those who (whether in a NHS or an independent sector institution) give professional treatment as part of a team, the patient having been referred within the team from medical to paramedical practitioner. In the former case paramedical practitioners acting independently would no doubt be in the same position as the doctors in the two cases discussed, since they would be acting as principals in the treatment. In the nature of the treatment likely to be involved, however, it is probable that opportunities to refrain from disclosure so as to avoid the adverse effect of worry on the proposed treatment will be considerably fewer than in the case of medical treatment.

By contrast, in the case of paramedical treatment given within a team, it is suggested that a paramedical practitioner would be most unwise and often positively wrong to give a false or misleading answer in response to a patient's inquiry about risks in proposed treatment. Overall responsibility for any deliberate concealment of risks to avoid the adverse effects of worry on treatment will no doubt rest with the medical practitioner in charge of the team treating the patient. Paramedical members of that team will be wise to check what the medical practitioner has told the inquiring patient about inherent risks. An even greater responsibility would appear to rest with the medical practitioner to keep other members of the treatment team informed in this respect. Prudence would indicate that any deliberate concealment for therapeutic reasons should be communicated to all those within a team with whom the patient is likely to have contact.

Information volunteered to patients

Even if a patient does not specifically make any inquiry about proposed treatment, it is nevertheless necessary in cases involving sane and conscious adults to explain the general nature and purpose of the treatment, for an action for battery to be avoided. The further question then arises as to whether any disclosure, and if so what, should be volunteered to the non-inquiring patient in respect of risks involved in the treatment.

On the one hand, a risk might on some occasions be so great and obvious that a failure to disclose it to a patient might be regarded as a failure to explain the very nature and purpose of the treatment. If so, any physical contact on the basis of such an inadequate explanation would be a battery, and the patient would be able to sue the practitioner responsible without any need to prove fault. It is sufficient if the physical contact is made, for the legal wrong to be committed.

On the other hand, if the risk involved is minimal, a warning to the patient might be positively harmful by causing greater consternation than was merited. It might, for instance, cause the patient to refuse treatment even though the disadvantages of such refusal far outweigh the very small risk involved.

As in the case of patients who specifically inquire whether the proposed treatment or procedure involves risk, few cases have been decided in this country on the disclosure required to be made to patients who make no such inquiry. Until recently, such decisions as there were involved the question, not of what risks ought to be volunteered to a patient, but rather the question whether any risks at all need to be disclosed in order to obtain a valid consent.

Opportunities for the patient's self-determination tend to become subsumed within the concept of clinical judgement or accepted medical practice, leaving it to the professionals to make the decision. Adoption of accepted medical practice as the guiding standard for disclosure tends to assume that it is only medical consideration which would weigh with the patient in arriving at an informed and rational decision.

The first English case to move on to consider the further question of which risks ought to be disclosed was *Chatterton v. Gerson* (1981), where the facts were as follows:

The plaintiff was a middle-aged woman who underwent a hernia operation. She later suffered pain at the operation site caused by a trapped nerve. Injections of local anaesthetic gave only temporary relief, and the pain became intractable. She was referred to a specialist in the treatment of intractable pain who gave her an injection to block the sensory nerve which transmitted the pain signals from the scar site to the brain. This was a last resort treatment which some doctors do not use. A second injection was given after the first failed to have more than a temporary effect. The plaintiff not only continued to experience acute agony in the scar area but also lost the feeling in her right leg. Her mobility was considerably impaired as a result, and she alleged that the doctor had wrongfully failed to give her an explanation of the procedures and their implications so that she could make an informed decision whether to risk them.

Her action alleged both trespass to the person (battery) and negligence. The battery action was dismissed, Mr Justice Bristow holding that once a patient has been informed in broad terms of the nature of the intended treatment and has given his consent, the patient cannot then say there has been a lack of real consent. The decision is of greater importance, however, in respect of the plaintiff's allegation that the doctor had negligently failed to give an explanation of the risks inherent in the proposed treatment.

The judge held that a doctor is required, as part of his duty of care to his patient, to explain what he intends to do, and the implications involved, in the way in which a responsible doctor in similar circumstances would do. If there is a real risk of misfortune inherent in the procedure, however well it is carried out, the doctor's duty is to warn of such misfortune. On all the evidence in this case the judge found that the defendant doctor had in fact carried out his duty to inform the plaintiff of the implications of the treatment. Numbness was not a foreseeable risk of the operation and the defendant was therefore not required to warn the plaintiff of that possibility.

The decision that a doctor must warn of 'real' or 'foreseeable' risks still leaves open the question of who is to judge what is real and what is foreseeable. The concept of foreseeability is a well-used legal concept distinguishing consequences which may reasonably be envisaged from mere outside chances. It would appear that the decision as to what risks are 'real' and 'foreseeable' will probably be left to professional judgement as part of the overall duty of care owed by practitioner to patient.

Mr Justice Bristow decided also that, even if the doctor had not in fact warned the plaintiff of the implications of the treatment, she had failed to prove that if she had been properly informed she would have refused to undergo the treatment and the risks involved. She was so desperate for pain relief that she would probably have gone ahead anyway. The plaintiff thus failed to prove the essential causal relationship between the alleged failure to explain and the resulting harm, in the shape of the materialisation of the risk. As was explained in Chapter 7 (p. 112) it is essential to the success of a negligence action that the breach of duty caused the damage complained of. If the patient would have gone ahead with the proposed treatment even after an explanation, that essential causal link between breach of duty and damage is lacking and a negligence action is bound to fail.

Parents, minors and children

The only person who can give valid and binding consent to treatment of a sane and conscious adult is that person himself. No one else may do so. It may happen that during consciousness an adult invests another person with the power of proxy consent, to be exercised on his behalf when he is incapable of giving consent himself. A person invested with the power of proxy consent must use it reasonably on behalf of the person who gave the power and must not unreasonably withhold consent when it is necessary or highly advisable.

Much the commonest instance, however, of the exercise of the power of proxy consent on behalf of another is the case of parents consenting to treatment of their children. The category of minors (those aged under 18 years) must be divided for present purposes into minors aged over 16 and minors and children below that age.

Section 8(1) of the Family Law Reform Act 1969 sets the age of valid independent consent to medical treatment at 16:

> The consent of a minor who has attained the age of 16 years to any surgical medical or dental treatment which, in the absence of consent, would constitute a trespass to his person, shall be as effective as it would be if he were of full age; and where a minor has by virtue of this section given an effective consent to any treatment it shall not be necessary to obtain any consent for it from his parent or guardian.

'Medical treatment' will of course include also paramedical treatment. The position is therefore that a parent of a minor aged 16 or more has no power of veto in respect of any necessary or desirable treatment to which the minor is willing to consent.

Section 8(3) of the 1969 Act goes on to state that:

> Nothing in this section shall be construed as making ineffective any consent which would have been effective had this section not been enacted.

Two possible interpretations may be placed on this subsection. The first is that a minor aged less than 16 may still give a valid independent consent to treatment if he or she is sufficiently mature and comprehending to understand the nature and purpose of what is proposed. The second is that the parent's common law right to consent to treatment on behalf of a minor aged more than 16 but less than 18 is unaffected.

Two sides of the question of the treatment of minors require consideration. One aspect involves the question of refusal of parental consent to treatment when the child or minor is willing to submit to it, or expresses no view about it, or is too young to be capable of doing so. The other aspect involves the question of a parent's wishing treatment to proceed when the minor refuses to submit to it.

Dealing first with the refusal of parental consent to treatment, it has already been noted that no parent has the power to veto treatment to which a minor aged 16 or more is willing to submit. The refusal of a parent to consent to treatment on a minor or child aged under 16 is more problematical. It appears that a distinction may usefully be drawn here between treatment which is immediately necessary to save life, preserve health or prevent present pain and suffering, and treatment which is desirable but not necessary for any of these purposes.

An oft-quoted example of parental refusal of consent to treatment which is considered medically necessary is the case of refusal of consent to blood transfusion when parent and child belong to a religious group which conscientiously objects to such treatment. There are various ways in which the necessary treatment could be justified or at least excused, although it should be emphasised that legal justifications should not lightly override deeply-held beliefs merely because those beliefs happen to be shared among only a small minority of people.

The former practice of taking children into care in such circumstances so that the local authority can authorise the proposed procedure has fallen out of favour and DHSS advice recommends hospital staff to exercise their clinical judgement in each case. Even if treatment of a child or minor under 16 in the face of a parental objection were technically to be held to be a battery, the damages would be likely to be extremely small if the treatment was immediately necessary to prevent loss of life or grave injury to health.

Indeed, a parent refusing necessary medical treatment for a sick child may be convicted of ill-treatment under section 1(1) of the Children and Young Persons Act 1933, and for manslaughter if the child were to die in consequence of neglect. It could be argued, further, that in giving treatment which is immediately necessary to preserve a child's life or health or to prevent or reduce present pain and suffering, the practitioner giving the treatment is giving no more than the child's parents are legally obliged to provide if they are not to be adjudged guilty of neglect. If the under-16-year-old minor in question were in a particular case to be mature and comprehending enough to understand the proposed treatment and were to consent, the problem would be greatly eased if not altogether removed.

If, however, the proposed treatment or procedure can safely be deferred without the danger of immediate harm to the child, it will be unwise in most cases and unlawful in some to proceed with treatment in the face of parental objection. In this case also, the problem would be eased if not removed if the minor was mature enough to understand the nature and purpose of the proposed treatment.

In the matter of what is immediately necessary to preserve life and health and prevent present suffering, and what is not immediately necessary (or perhaps not necessary at all but only desirable) courts will naturally be influenced by clinical judgement exercised in accordance with widely or generally accepted practice.

Common considerations apply in these respects to both medical and paramedical practitioners. In paramedical practice, however, the incidence of cases involving an immediate need to intervene to preserve health or to prevent pain, and the likelihood of parental refusal of consent, will be relatively much smaller than in medical practice.

The second aspect of the problem of consent by and on behalf of minors involves the situation in which a parent is willing for treatment to proceed but the minor objects. This problem may itself be subdivided into three cases: the case of the minor aged 16 or over; the case of the mature and comprehending minor under 16; and the child who is too young to comprehend, but who may nevertheless object because he does not like what is happening.

In the third case it seems that a parent may give valid consent to treatment of a child provided the treatment is not actually against the child's interests.[1] This is a wider test than that of treatment in the best interests of the child. In the other two cases, in which the minor is capable of giving and therefore refusing consent because he or she is over 16 or is mature and comprehending, practitioners would generally be unwise to rely on parental consent in face of a clear objection from the minor. While each case must be considered in the light of its own particular circumstances, a comprehending refusal should probably be given as much weight as would be given to a comprehending consent in other contexts. Just as parents have no right to veto treatment of a consenting minor over 16, neither ought they to be able to act against such a person's refusal of treatment. In the case of minors under 16, parental insistence in the face of a minor's objection might be ignored if the minor were sufficiently mature and comprehending, or at least confined to cases of clear benefit to the minor.

Treating the mentally disordered

Some patients suffering from mental disorder may be perfectly volitional and capable of consenting to treatment. Others, for instance the severely mentally retarded, will be quite unable to give independent consent. In the case of many detained patients, section 63 of the Mental Health Act 1983 enables certain treatment for mental disorder to be given without consent. As regards paramedical practice, such treatment might for instance take the form of therapy designed to alleviate the patient's mental condition. The treatment must be given under the direction of the responsible medical officer in charge of the mental patient's treatment.

Certain treatments may require the approval of an independent medical practitioner appointed under the Mental Health Act 1983 if they are lawfully to be given without the consent of the patient. These treatments include electroconvulsive therapy, and drug treatment if three months or more have elapsed since drugs were first given during that period of detention. Before issuing a certificate that the proposed treatment is appropriate the appointed medical practitioner must consult a nurse and one other person (neither a nurse nor a doctor) who has been professionally concerned with the patient's treatment. Such a person might be a therapist who has been involved with the treatment of the patient in question. It is emphasised that the treatment which is the subject of this comment is treatment for the patient's mental disorder; treatment for physical illness, even in a mentally disordered patient, remains subject to the normal common law rules discussed earlier. The consultation just referred to is also required in the case of psychosurgery and hormone implants where, however, the patient's consent is always needed as well.

So far as paramedical treatment for the cure or alleviation of a physical condition is concerned, detained patients and voluntary patients appear to stand on the same footing. A volitional and comprehending patient may refuse to participate in the treatment or therapy, and in such a case it will be unwise to exercise anything more than firm persuasion to encourage co-operation. So far as non-volitional and non-comprehending patients are concerned, treatment and therapy would appear to be lawfully permitted if given in their 'best interests'. Even an apparent objection might be ignored if staff consider that the patient does not really comprehend what he is saying.

If an operation or any other substantial procedure is being considered, the consent of the incomprehending patient's nearest relative might wisely be sought as a safeguard additional to that of acting in the 'best interests' of the patient. However, given the relatively small degree of physical interference involved in most instances of remedial therapy, the paramedical practitioner will normally be able to rely on the 'best interests' principle alone.

Unconscious patients

There are occasions on which certain paramedical practitioners are called upon to perform procedures upon an unconscious patient. For fullness of reference, brief mention of the governing principle is now given.

Treatment of unconscious patients will normally be given with the consent of the nearest available relative if possible. In the absence of any such person, treatment will be lawfully permitted if it is designed to save life, to avoid the immediate risk of serious damage to health, or to prevent the risk of pain and suffering.

Consent and research

A statement issued by the Medical Research Council in 1962 [2] gives valuable guidance on the use of patients in research, experimental treatment and controlled trials. The statement distinguishes in particular between procedures contributing to the benefit of the individual and procedures which are of no direct benefit. In relation to beneficial procedures it states:

> In the case of procedures directly connected with the management of the condition in the particular individual, the relationship is essentially that between doctor and patient. Implicit in this relationship is the willingness on the part of the subject to be guided by the judgement of his medical attendant.

Provided the 'medical attendant' (which term may for present purposes be extended to cover paramedical practitioners) is satisfied that there are reasonable grounds for thinking that the new procedure in question will benefit the patient, the consent of the patient should be evaluated and assessed on the same basis as if the treatment were part of established practice. This advice must now be read subject to the recent introduction (p. 158) of the requirement to volunteer an explanation of the 'real' risks to the patient.

It therefore follows, continues the statement,

> that it is clearly within the competence of a parent or guardian of a child to give permission for procedures intended to benefit that child when he is not old or intelligent enough to be able himself to give a valid consent.

In the case of procedures which are of no direct benefit to the individual sought to be made the subject of research, the Medical

Research Council's statement stresses that it is 'always necessary to ensure that the true consent of the subject is explicitly obtained'.

It is clear enough that a patient's implied consent to experimental treatment which is of no direct benefit to him cannot be assumed merely from the fact that he has entered a teaching hospital. Express consent will be just as necessary in such a situation as it is elsewhere. The Medical Research Council's statement remains, with the wisdom of hindsight, somewhat incomplete when it describes the express consent needed for experimental treatment having no direct benefit to the patient thus:

> By true consent is meant consent freely given and with proper understanding of the nature and consequences of what is proposed.

'Nature and consequences' clearly goes further than 'nature and purpose' and involves the need to explain risks. If consent to therapeutic treatment now requires an explanation of 'real' risks, the necessary consent in cases of procedures not directly benefiting the patient must surely be based on an explanation even of small risks, and possibly of all risks which are known to the person seeking consent for experimental treatment.

Finally, in relation to the use of patients in controlled trials, the statement says:

> Such trials are . . . only feasible when it is possible to compare suitable groups of patients and only permissible when there is a genuine doubt within the profession as to which of two treatments or preventive regimes is the better. In these circumstances it is justifiable to give to a proportion of the patients the novel procedure on the understanding that the remainder receive the procedure previously accepted as the best. In the case where no effective treatment has previously been devised then the situation should be fully explained to the participants and their true consent obtained.

When the statement refers to 'true' consent it again appears that it should today be interpreted to refer not only to 'real' risks, which should be volunteered in an ordinary therapeutic situation, but also lesser and possibly all known risks inherent in the experimental procedure or treatment. Furthermore, given that the objectives of a controlled trial might be both therapeutic and non-therapeutic, it may sensibly be suggested that the obligation to disclose and explain known risks increases in proportion to the extent that the patient involved in the trial is unlikely to derive direct benefit from it.

In the case of research involving children the statement explains:

> In the strict view of the law parents and guardians of minors cannot give consent on their behalf to any procedures which are of no particular benefit to them and which may carry some risks of harm.

As for the minor being able to consent independently of a parent or guardian, the statement adds that

> it may safely be assumed that the Courts will not regard a child of 12 years or under (or 14 years or under for boys in Scotland) as having the capacity to consent to any procedure which may involve him in an injury. Above this age the reality of any purported consent which may have been obtained is a question of fact and as with an adult the evidence would, if necessary, have to show that irrespective of age the person concerned fully understood the implications to himself of the procedures to which he was consenting.

In the case of persons who are mentally disordered or retarded, when 'true' consent (as explained above) cannot be obtained, procedures which are of no direct benefit and which might carry a risk of harm to the subject of the proposed research should not be undertaken.

THE PRINCIPLE OF CONFIDENTIALITY

Confidentiality, containing as it does elements of both trust and secrecy, lies at the very root of the treatment relationship. As such it is a fundamental axiom of medical practice that doctors shall regard themselves as generally bound to maintain silence about what has been confided to them during the process of medical consultation. The principle of confidentiality is equally fundamental to paramedical practice, though its particular dictates are apt to vary according to the relationship of the paramedical practitioner both to the medical profession and to the patient or client.

Given that paramedical practitioners are frequently involved as members of a treatment team, the question naturally arises as to how far, if at all, confidentiality should be maintained even vis-à-vis the other members of the team, including the medical members. Of course, no rule can be laid down in advance about what information to share with a colleague, particularly a colleague who is also involved in the treatment of the same patient. But guidance may always be derived from an indication of the reason for which confidentiality should be preserved.

The principle of confidentiality exists first and foremost for the benefit of the patient. It may also be of frequent assistance to practitioners whose convenience is suited to preserve a silence about what has passed between them and their patients or clients. But that is a secondary consequence of the confidentiality principle and not its primary purpose. If, then, patient benefit is of the essence, a natural corollary would seem to be that disclosure of confidential information is justified if it will serve the patient's best interests.

Disclosure of much information about a patient, particularly information relating to treatment, will have to be made to colleagues within a treatment team. The same consideration applies also to communications between a referring medical or dental practitioner and the paramedical practitioner to whom the patient is referred. It can therefore be assumed that disclosure within such relationships can be justified without the need to obtain consent from the patient. If a patient expresses an objection to any such disclosure, problems may arise as to how the patient's interests are to be balanced.

Just as in the case of consent to treatment, so too in the case of the confidentiality of information, patient self-determination should be fundamental. In the case of consent, it was seen in the first section of this chapter that self-determination remains a long way from being paramount. Does self-determination fare any better when it comes to considering the question of confidentiality? The answer is that although self-determination is in some respects a guiding principle, in many others it fares no better than it did in the case of consent to treatment.

If, in particular, confidentiality is to be based on the 'best interests' of the patient, then other factors may rank with equal importance alongside the principle when it comes to considering what is really best for the patient. Indeed, the BMA *Handbook of Medical Ethics* lists disclosure in the interests of the patient as a justifiable exception to the principle of confidentiality.

Confidentiality and discipline

Practitioners in every branch of paramedical practice may encounter confidential information about patients and clients, whether it be directly connected with treatment or diagnosis, or in the form of casual remarks or statements unconnected with the treatment itself.

In view of their assistance with diagnosis, it is hardly surprising that registered radiographers and registered medical laboratory scientific officers should find included in the statements of 'infamous conduct in a professional respect' the following statement, common to both. Neither shall

> Knowingly disclose to any patient or to any other unauthorised person, the result of any investigations or any other information of a personal or confidential nature gained in the course of practice of his/her profession.

Apart from the natural prohibition contained in the latter part of the rule, it is interesting to note the prohibition against disclosing the result of investigations to the patient himself. This additional restriction serves to underline the supplementary responsibilities which paramedical practitioners owe to the medical profession. In the case of both medical laboratory scientific officers and radiographers the principal diagnostic responsibility lies with the medical practitioner in charge of the patient's treatment.

Exceptions to the principle

Disclosure 'in the interests of the patient' has already been noted as an exception to the obligation to maintain confidentiality. An even clearer and indeed more pressing reason for disclosure of what might otherwise have remained secret is that the patient or client actually requests disclosure of the information in question. It might occasionally be in the patient's best interests to request permission to disclose certain information, but in many cases the better course may be to refrain from seeking such permission. In the case of a specific request or instruction from a patient to disclose, however, it must be assumed that a patient in his right senses knows what is best for him.

The case of *C.v.C.* (1946), involving a medical practitioner but equally authoritative in the paramedical context, lays down the proposition that a desire to avoid doing anything to infringe the confidential relationship between doctor and patient, though an important consideration, does not justify a doctor in refusing to divulge confidential information to any named person or persons when asked by the patient so to do. The privilege of the patient may thus be waived, and it is not then open to the doctor to refuse disclosure.

A paramedical practitioner is in the same position when faced with a specific request to disclose. Moreover, there could be circumstances in which a paramedical practitioner could be guilty of negligence in failing to relay information to a third party in response to such a request if the failure resulted in harm to the patient. This may be an additional, though less likely, possibility to that of failure to relay to another member of the treatment team a piece of vital information about the patient or his condition, resulting in harm or injury. This latter omission would consist of a failure to act in the patient's best interests, those interests having been noted above as the basis of justifiable disclosure.

A further exception to the principle of confidentiality occurs where the information is required to be divulged by 'due process of law'. Or at least, this is a case where, by definition, a legal justification for breach of confidence is provided even if some might in certain cases say that legal obligation to disclose by no means concludes the question of the ethical justification of such disclosure. Paramedical practitioners will hardly be surprised at the statutory duty imposed on 'any person' to provide information under the Prevention of Terrorism (Temporary Provisions) Act 1976, though some might find the similar duty in respect of the investigation of road accidents rather less in accord with their ethical responsibilities, as did a doctor in a case reported in 1974.

In *Hunter v. Mann* (1974) a medical practitioner treated a man at his evening surgery. The man asked Dr Hunter to visit his girl friend who said that she had been in a car accident. The doctor advised them both to inform the police but did not ask their consent to disclose their identity if asked to do so. It transpired that on the same day a stolen car had been involved in an accident and that the driver and passenger had run away immediately afterwards. The doctor was visited three weeks later by police who requested the name and address of either or both the patients or information leading to their identification.

The doctor refused and was convicted of an offence under the Road Traffic Act 1972, section 168(2)(b) of which states that any person shall be required to give any information which it is in his power to give and which may lead to the identification of the driver. Dr Hunter was found guilty of a criminal offence, but his ethics remained intact. His fine, moreover, was a mere £5.

More generally, paramedical practitioners may be made compellable witnesses by subpoena or witness summons procedures noted in the following chapter (p. 177) in relation to evidence generally. There is neither medical nor paramedical professional privilege enabling a practitioner to refuse to answer a question as a witness in court. Nor is there any privilege against the production of records and case notes which are in the practitioner's possession, custody or control. It is noted in the following chapter (p. 191) that while there is no medical or paramedical professional privilege to withhold evidence when instructed by a court to give it, judges may be favourably disposed to a practitioner who is unwilling to disclose on grounds of professional conscience. But any such favourable attitude must yield to the need to disclose when the matters to be disclosed are essential to the proceedings.

Refusal to comply with a court order to give evidence or to produce documents amounts to contempt of court and is a criminal offence punishable with a fine or, in serious cases, imprisonment. One device which practitioners sometimes use when they do not wish to volunteer confidential information to a court is to ask the judge to make a ruling whether or not the information in question should be disclosed. If the ruling is that disclosure should be made, the practitioner may feel that he or she can go ahead with a clear conscience.

Social duty to disclose

Much the widest of the commonly accepted exceptions to the duty to maintain confidentiality of patient information lies in what is described as an 'overriding social duty' which transcends the interests of the patient or client and which may therefore justifiably displace it. It is not possible in advance to set out the circumstances in which social duty may justifiably override duty to the individual. As a general rule, however, it may safely be assumed that the prevention of avoidable or foreseeable harm to others is a sufficient reason for overriding the interests of the patient in confidentiality. Where harm to the patient himself is envisaged, disclosure may be justified on the ground of the patient's own 'best interests' mentioned earlier.

The practical problem arises, if disclosure seems to be in the paramount public interest, as to which course to adopt in making the information known. In cases, for instance, of conditions which make a patient unfit to drive the question arises whether to inform the vehicle licensing authority directly or to seek to persuade the patient to disclose the relevant condition himself, as indeed he has a legal duty to do. In the latter case the practitioner will be free of any question of censure because the disclosure has been made as a result of the patient's own independent choice. The right to confidentiality has been waived by the patient's own disclosure.

The converse aspect of this situation raises the question whether a practitioner who knows that a patient or client may cause harm to others or has committed a serious offence will be guilty of any legal wrong if that information is kept secret. The fear is sometimes voiced by practitioners that they may be guilty, for instance, of aiding and abetting a criminal offence simply by omitting to reveal it to the responsible authority, normally the police. Practitioners can at once be assured that they will not be at the slightest risk of prosecution for merely omitting to disclose information in such cases, still less for actually aiding and abetting the offence committed by the patient or client.

A further question arises as to civil liability resulting from non-disclosure. If, for instance, a practitioner were not to pursue the morally justifiable and no doubt morally indicated course of informing the vehicle licensing authority about a patient's unfitness to drive, would the practitioner be liable for negligence if the patient injured a third party as a result of the condition or disability known to the practitioner? It seems improbable in the present state of the law that any such liability would be entailed. The law does not generally impose a positive duty to act for the benefit of another, unless there is a special relationship between the parties in question. A practitioner clearly owes a positive duty to a patient or client to act in that person's best interests. The person injured as a result of the patient's condition or disability in the present example is not, however, a party to the practitioner-patient relationship.

Nevertheless it is not inconceivable that the law of negligence might at some future time be extended to impose liability upon a practitioner towards an injured third party in these circumstances. The legal duty to the patient himself will no doubt be satisfied by a clear warning of the dangers of driving (or of whatever other course of action is proposed) with the condition or disability which the practitioner has explained to the patient.

Cases of suspected child abuse may raise special problems. If the child in question is himself a patient of the practitioner there is no problem about the ethical justification of disclosure, since the practitioner would be acting in the patient's own best interests. In other cases there is no doubt a social duty to disclose reasonable suspicions of child abuse to a responsible authority, say to the local authority social services department or to the NSPCC.

Where a paramedical practitioner comes by information leading to suspicion of child abuse in his or her capacity as a member of a treatment team, it will normally be wise to channel any such information through the person in charge of the team rather than to act independently. Both medical and paramedical practitioners will be reassured in the event of any such disclosure by the decision of the House of Lords in the case of *D. v. NSPCC* (1977).

Their Lordships held that the public interest requires those who give information about child abuse to the society should be immune from disclosure of their identity in legal proceedings. If this were not so, said their Lordships, the society's sources of information would dry up. In this sort of case, however, the primary consideration appears not to be that of maintaining confidentiality but of seeking the best available means of protecting the public interest in the prevention of child abuse. Their Lordships added that the fact that information has been communicated by one person to another in confidence is not of itself a sufficient ground for protecting from disclosure in a court of law the nature of the information or the identity of the informant if either of these matters would assist the court to ascertain facts which are relevant to an issue on which it is adjudicating.

Requests for information

Paramedical practitioners should exercise care in responding to requests from third parties for information relating to their patients or clients. Relaying the results of an examination for, say, purposes of accident compensation to a solicitor who states in writing that he is acting on behalf of the patient presents no problem. But special care must be taken to avoid disclosure of information to anyone who might be acting for another person and possibly adversely to the patient's interests. If in any doubt the practitioner should seek the patient's consent to disclosure in which case the privilege attaching to confidentiality of information will be waived. If a patient positively requests the relay of information to a third party then the practitioner is under a duty to comply with the request, as in the case of *C.v.C.* (1946) mentioned above (p. 167).

The justification of disclosure of information can usually be assumed in the case of inquiries from a spouse as to the patient's condition, unless of course the patient has forbidden any such disclosure. Furthermore, great care should be taken in any case in which information might be likely to affect the marital relationship between the inquiring spouse and the patient. One such case is mentioned below, under the heading of remedies for breach of confidence.

Remedies for breach of confidence

It is frequently assumed that, quite apart from any disciplinary consequences which might flow from an unjustified breach of confidence, an action for damages will be available to the aggrieved party. It may well be that the law will provide such an action at some future time, but the cases decided to date are confined to breaches of confidence involving the unjustified disclosure of information having a commercial value.

An injunction to prevent further disclosure may be granted at the court's discretion. But such a remedy is of no avail if the damage has already been done. It will be too little and too late. If an injunction is obtained by the applicant, any further breach by the other party in the form of repetition of the information in question is a contempt of court and a criminal offence.

Although, as already noted, it cannot be said that in its present state the law will award damages in respect of unjustifiable disclosure of personal as distinct from commercial information, there is judicial authority to the effect that an action for damages is available if the unjustifiable disclosure causes the aggrieved party to suffer nervous shock in the sense of injury to health as distinct from mere upset or distress.

Testimonials and references

Defamation is the publication of a false statement which reflects on a person's reputation and has the effect of lowering him in the estimation of right thinking people. A reference will not be defamatory if its contents are true and accurate even if the motive behind it is spiteful.

Even if a reference or testimonial contains a false statement, then provided it was written with care and in good faith it will be protected against a defamation action by qualified privilege. Care must be taken to communicate the reference only to those who are properly concerned with its contents. A person may be liable for the publication of a defamatory statement if he ought to have foreseen that the reference would be read by someone not having a legitimate interest in its contents. In case of doubt the circulation of testimonials and references should be restricted by marking the envelope 'personal', 'private', 'confidential' or similarly. It is no excuse that the letter was addressed to the wrong person in the mistaken belief that he or she was privileged to receive it.

REFERENCES

[1] See Skegg: *Consent to Medical Procedures on Minors*, (1973) 36 M.L.R. 370, p. 381

[2] *Responsibility in Investigation on Human Subjects*. In the Report of the Medical Research Council 1962–3 (Cmnd. 2382). (A revised version of this document is in preparation at the time of writing.)

Chapter Ten

EVIDENCE AND DISCLOSURE OF RECORDS

GIVING EVIDENCE

The ways in which practitioners in a profession supplementary to medicine may become involved in legal proceedings are many and various. In the particular matter of giving evidence, a broad distinction may be drawn between two capacities in which it is given. First, evidence may be given in a purely personal capacity. For instance, a practitioner may happen to witness an accident, in which he or she becomes involved simply as an onlooker and in no way as a person concerned with the treatment of the victim. Second, evidence may be given in a specialist capacity as an expert, in a case in which the practitioner's involvement arises not merely from chance encounter but from a professional relationship with a patient or client.

It is with this second capacity, the specialist professional capacity, that the contents of this chapter relating to evidence are concerned. Some introductory remarks applicable to evidence in general will be given for the sake of general reference and explanation. But the bulk of the information contained in this chapter relates specifically to evidence prepared and disclosed in a professional capacity.

DISCLOSURE OF RECORDS

This, the second item to be considered in this chapter, naturally has reference only to materials and records prepared by a practitioner in a professional capacity. The subject of disclosure of records fits well into a chapter concerned principally with matters of evidence. For in addition to actually appearing in court to give expert evidence on a subject of special expertise, practitioners may be called upon prior to such an occasion, or instead of it, to disclose to a party to legal proceedings such documents and records as that person, or his legal adviser, is able to require to be produced. It will be seen in the course of this chapter that the disclosure of documents and records for a variety of reasons prior to those proceedings can have an important and often vital bearing on those proceedings. Disclosure, or lack of it, may even affect the decision whether or not to commence or to continue the proceedings at all.

THE SCOPE OF EVIDENCE

Evidence is the way in which facts are proved. The law of evidence consists of those rules of law which are concerned with the way in which facts are proved in courts of law. The emphasis in these definitions on 'fact' is not without significance. For it will be seen in this chapter that an expert witness has an exceptional ability to testify to opinions as well as to facts. Admissibility of statements of opinion is, exceptionally, justified in certain cases. The principal such case is that of the expert witness. The role and function of the expert witness are considered shortly, and such consideration is naturally devoted almost entirely to expert medical and paramedical evidence.

Evidence may be oral, documentary or real. Oral evidence is self-explanatory, being the evidence spoken by a witness to a court in the course of legal proceedings. Documentary evidence is also self-explanatory, being papers and documents which are called in evidence as proof of facts to which they relate. The expression is sometimes encountered in relation to documentary evidence that it must be the 'best' evidence available. This means that the original of the document in question should, if it exists, be produced in evidence in preference to a copy of it, in cases where it is sought to prove the contents of the document.

This terminological usage should not be confused with what may, in broad terms, be the best or most helpful way of presenting evidence on a particular matter to a court. For instance, one situation to be discussed in this chapter concerns the desirability and sometimes also the necessity of adducing the oral evidence of expert witnesses in order to explain the sometimes complex or specialist terminology contained in medical reports. In many cases, however, documentary evidence alone may be sufficient, for instance in cases involving personal injuries caused by road accidents in which there is no dispute as to the contents of the medical report and no reason to believe a court would be likely to require further explanation of the contents of the report. Documentary evidence may include, for example, the written results of blood tests carried out for forensic purposes by medical laboratory scientific officers.

Real evidence means evidence in the form of things or objects. The familiar expression 'Exhibit A', referring to a weapon alleged to have been used in the commission of a criminal assault, is encountered in the giving of 'real' evidence. In a case in which the plaintiff has suffered physical injuries, a judge or jury may wish to see for themselves the extent of the injuries and the way in which, for instance, they have affected the plaintiff's movement. Examples of real evidence in cases requiring specialist medical or similar evidence would include an object removed from the victim of an accident or an assault, and an item such as a swab or instrument left inside a patient following a surgical operation.

Evidence may be direct or circumstantial. Direct evidence consists of statements as to what a witness has actually perceived. If such evidence is accepted this eliminates the necessity of drawing inferences from the evidence in order to find the alleged fact proved. By contrast, circumstantial evidence is evidence from which material facts may be inferred. It does not directly establish the existence or non-existence of the alleged facts, but rather it allows such facts to be inferred as a reasonable probability. For this reason it will be obvious that circumstantial evidence must always yield to available direct evidence of the facts in issue. Both direct evidence and circumstantial evidence may be given in an oral, documentary or real form.

CALLING WITNESSES

In respect of both individual and professional capacities the attendance at court of a practitioner is likely to be a voluntary matter. This will particularly be so when such a practitioner is requested by one side in a personal injuries action to attend and testify to matters within that person's special expertise. That is not to say, however, that means of the enforcement of such an expert's attendance at court do not exist. Quite the contrary, for both the High Court and the County Court have means at their disposal for requiring the attendance at the court of a person who it is thought might not otherwise attend. The enforcement procedures available respectively to the High Court and the County Court are applicable to both expert and non-expert witnesses.

The High Court has power, on the application of a party to proceedings who considers that a witness may not attend unless required to do so, to issue two types of writ against the unwilling witness. The writ of *subpoena ad testificandum* requires the attendance of the witness to testify, and a *subpoena duces tecum* requires the person to whom it is addressed not only to attend and give evidence but also to bring such documents in his possession as are considered material by the party making application for the writ.

Refusal to attend in the way directed by a High Court *subpoena* exposes the person in question to punishment for contempt of court. For the effects, which may be a fine or even imprisonment, a clear case of contempt must be made out. There is no contempt if there was a reasonable excuse, such as illness, for which the witness did not attend. Physical inability to travel has been held to be a legitimate excuse, but an employer's instruction was in one case held to be no excuse for non-attendance, even when it was framed in very strong terms.

Refusal to attend in response to a *subpoena* may also entitle the person who has obtained the *subpoena* to an action for damages against the non-attender. In the cases which have been decided on this matter, damages have been limited to the costs wasted by the other party owing to the witness's non-attendance. It is not necessary for the success of such an action for the plaintiff to prove that he had a good cause of action, nor that the absence of the witness was the only cause of losing the action.

The method of summoning witnesses in the County Court (for actions involving smaller amounts of money than those which must be heard in the High Court) is by witness summons. The procedure applies both to summoning a witness to give evidence and to summoning a witness to produce a document in his possession or control. The penalty for disobeying a witness summons is a fine. If such a fine is imposed the county court judge has power to direct that all or part of it, after deducting costs, is to be applicable towards indemnifying the party injured by the refusal or omission to comply with the witness summons.

In neither the High Court nor the County Court is a witness so instructed liable to attend unless he is paid expenses and an appropriate sum in respect of attendance. For attendance on a witness summons from the County Court the amounts payable are laid down in the

County Court Rules 1981,and in the case of a High Court *subpoena* the amount must be such as is reasonable bearing in mind especially the length of his probable stay at the place of trial. A professional witness who is called by *subpoena* to attend solely in order to give expert evidence, as distinct from evidence as to the facts of the case, may claim compensation for loss of time before giving his expert evidence.

Much the most usual way of ensuring the attendance at court of an expert witness is, however, by prior agreement with the person (or his legal advisers) requiring the expert evidence as proof of his case. Fees may be agreed in advance, and these will reflect the proper amount to be charged by a practitioner of the standing and experience of the practitioner in question. It may, however, happen in some instances that the court will disagree with the amount claimed and reduce it. This is more likely to happen in a case involving legal aid, in which the lawyers have a duty to conduct the case in the way which is most reasonably economical.[1]

BURDEN AND STANDARD OF PROOF

The burden of proof of a fact lies upon the party who alleges it. In a case involving a claim for damages for personal injuries, in respect of which expert medical or paramedical evidence may be called by one or other party, the legal burden of proof normally rests on the person claiming the damages. In an action for negligence the onus of proving that there has been a breach of a duty of care causing injury to the plaintiff lies upon the plaintiff. But if the defendant alleges contributory negligence on the part of the plaintiff and seeks for that reason to reduce his liability to pay damages, proof of alleged contributory negligence lies upon the defendant who raises the matter.

Distinguished from the legal burden is the evidential burden which may shift from one side to the other during the course of the trial. (The evidential burden is the burden of adducing sufficient evidence to raise a particular issue in the case or to justify a verdict in a party's favour.) Since it is for the person alleging that something happened to prove that it did, and not for the other party to the proceedings to prove that it did not, the evidential burden will rest initially on the party bearing the legal burden. But as the weight of evidence given by each side during the course of the trial varies, the evidential burden will shift to the party who would fail in the event of no further evidence being brought.

Sometimes a confusion is made between burden of proof and standard of proof. The burden rests in the way described above. The standard required to discharge that burden is a separate matter. The standard of proof resting on the prosecution in a criminal case is proof of the allegations beyond reasonable doubt. This high standard of proof is required because in a criminal case the liberty of the subject is in issue.

In civil cases involving liability for personal injuries the plaintiff must prove his case on the balance of probabilities. In effecting the balance one way or the other the court is considering whether the allegations are 'more probable than not' to be true. However, even in civil cases there is a principle that the graver the allegation, the higher will be the degree of proof (though it will not reach the standard required in criminal cases). Such a higher standard, greater than the mere balance of probabilities, is required when fraud is alleged in a civil case.

Cases involving allegations of professional misconduct before a disciplinary committee of one of the boards of the professions supplementary to medicine also require a higher standard of proof. In setting down a rule which is equally applicable to the professions supplementary to medicine, *Moore v. General Dental Council* (1964) is authority for the proposition that professional tribunals should not condemn on the balance of probabilities.

In considering whether the standard of proof required of the party making the allegation or claim has been sufficient, both the quality and the quantity of the evidence may be taken into account. But questions of fact are certainly not to be decided simply by counting the number of witnesses on each side.

JUDICIAL NOTICE

There are some facts which are the subject of 'judicial notice' and which therefore require no proof. Among such facts are included statutes passed since 1850 and every branch of English law including also international law and EEC law. More relevant for present purposes is information falling under the heading of 'notorious facts'. Such information, which is common knowledge and need not be proved, includes certain facts of human life and existence.

It is common knowledge, for instance, that a man who has never been in the company of a woman cannot be the father of her child (except in the case of artificial insemination). It is also common knowledge that it is impossible for a child to be born alive after only two weeks of gestation. Impossibility, must however, be distinguished from improbability.

A judge, a magistrate or a member of a tribunal may use his general knowledge of local affairs and conditions in order to equip himself to take judicial notice of a fact, further proof of which will not then be required. A paramedical or medical practitioner who is a member of a bench or tribunal is not entitled to use his particular knowledge of the case before it.

In contrast, however, some cases may not involve knowledge of the particular case but rather specialist knowledge affecting the medical background to the case. An example is the case of *Wetherall v. Harrison* (1976). In that case a motorist was given a breath test which proved positive and was taken to a police station, where the appropriate procedure was followed. He could not produce a second specimen of urine within an hour of the first and so elected to give a specimen of blood, as being the only alternative. His behaviour then changed and he appeared to be having a fit, causing the blood sample to be unable to be taken. The police surgeon could not find any medical abnormalities, and the man was charged with failing without reasonable excuse to provide a specimen for a laboratory test, contrary to section 9(3) of the Road Traffic Act 1972.

In his evidence before the magistrates the police surgeon ruled out all medical reasons for the man's behaviour and said he thought the man had been simulating a fit. One of the magistrates was a general medical practitioner, and in the retiring room he gave his colleagues his medical opinion on the medical evidence of the police surgeon relating to the issue whether the fit was simulated or genuine. The other magistrates also had wartime experience of innoculations and the fear which they could create in certain people. They acquitted the man after taking the view that his fit was genuine and not simulated, and that therefore he had a reasonable excuse for failing to provide a specimen.

On appeal by the prosecution on a point of law to the Divisional Court the magistrates were held to have acted properly. It was not improper, the court held, for a magistrate with special knowledge of circumstances which merely formed the background to a particular case to draw on that specialised knowledge for the purpose of interpreting the evidence. The case is different from one in which he is in fact giving evidence to himself and to the other members of the bench.

This case is of interest to any paramedical practitioner engaged in tribunal work or service as a magistrate, in so far as it sets a distinction between specialist (or non-specialist) knowledge of the facts of a particular case, and specialist knowledge which simply forms the background for interpreting the evidence adduced.

THE EXPERT WITNESS

Witnesses are normally called to testify to matters of fact relating to the case in hand, and not to offer the court their opinion. But an exception exists in the case of an expert witness, called on to give evidence on scientific or technical matters. Practitioners in professions supplementary to medicine are therefore apt to be asked (or in more unusual cases required by the court) to give evidence according to their own particular expertise and specialty.

It may indeed happen that a practitioner is called upon to testify both as to fact and as to expert opinion, in a case in which he or she has a direct connection (say as a witness to events) with the matter in issue. In the absence of any such direct connection the court will be unlikely to require an expert to testify if such evidence would involve a breach of confidence.

An expert witness will have made a special study of the subject upon which evidence is to be given, though such knowledge need not have been acquired in any professional capacity. It is possible for students, trainees and even unqualified practitioners to be called to testify as to their expert opinion. Less weight would, of course, be given to such evidence than would be given to that of a qualified and experienced practitioner.

An expert should present his expert evidence in a clear, planned and comprehensible sequence. Steps taken to reach a particular conclusion should be explained, and the conclusion itself should not be left as a bare statement. This is because the expert, even though giving an opinion to the court, should not be seen to usurp the ultimate function of the court itself to express an opinion as to the outcome of the case.

Two points on medical and paramedical negligence arise here. In a case in which the expert witness is giving an opinion about medical or paramedical treatment or conduct, where, say, an injured patient alleges negligence against a practitioner, expert evidence is certainly admissible as to whether the treatment in question was orthodox (*Collier v. Simpson* (1831)). But the practitioner witness must not go further and give an opinion as to whether the treatment was negligent. For that decision is for the court itself to make (*Rich v. Pierpont* (1862)).

Nor will a court admit evidence from an expert witness if such evidence in fact does no more than rehearse the arguments as to blame or causation in respect of an accident. Again, liability is a question for the court to decide and evidence from an expert as to the proper outcome of the case is inadmissible. To be admissible as evidence the expert opinion should confine itself to specialist technical matters upon which the court itself can base its own conclusions.

Expert evidence may, except with the court's permission or where all parties agree, be given only when the person wishing to adduce such evidence has applied under the Rules of the Supreme Court for directions as to the introduction and exchange between the parties to the action of such evidence. In 1980 the Rules of the Supreme Court were amended to make leave to introduce expert evidence in most personal injury actions automatic. Experts are, under this automatic procedure, limited to two medical (or paramedical) witnesses and one non-medical witness for each side. The automatic procedure, containing as it does the limitation on the number of witnesses, does not apply in the case of actions involving allegations of negligence against a medical or paramedical practitioner. This latter type of case is discussed separately later in the chapter.

EXPERT TESTIMONY IN GENERAL

For reasons which will become clear, an expert opinion should be clearly presented, methodical, fully detailed and explained, and most certainly unbiased. A seasoned and experienced judge may well be averse to evidence which has clearly been slanted in the particular direction favourable to the party on whose behalf it is given. Of course, if the expert evidence speaks for itself and is in any event favourable to the plaintiff claiming damages or to the defendant seeking to resist or reduce them, that is another matter altogether.

Good and unbiased presentation are of particular importance in practice when, for instance, lawyers acting for a defendant in a personal injuries action pay a certain sum of money into court. This is done when they admit liability or consider their client may be made liable when the issue is tried. The amount of any such sum is not known to the judge. If, in the event, the judge finds the defendant liable for the accident (or if liability has in any event been admitted) and awards a sum smaller than that which has been paid into court, the plaintiff must pay the costs of both sides, maybe a large amount. It is clearly important that the presentation and form of expert evidence on his behalf should not of itself prejudice the case.

EXAMINATION OF WITNESSES IN COURT

Oral evidence in court must be given either on oath or on affirmation. A witness who objects to taking an oath may base his objection on religious grounds or upon the fact that he holds no religious views. No other ground of objection is allowed.

The examination of a witness begins with the examination in chief, and leading questions are not permitted except in respect of the name, address and occupation of the witness or of facts which are not in dispute. A leading question is a question which is put in a way which suggests the answer desired by counsel putting the question.

Cross-examination by the other side may attempt to question or weaken the other party's case, by diminishing the weight to be attached to the witness's evidence. In the case of an expert witness, questions may be put in cross-examination which test experience and extent of knowledge. Thus at this stage a judge, or jury if the particular case is of a type which requires one, will begin the process of balancing the relative weight of the respective sets of evidence. In cross-examination leading questions are permitted to be put to the witness.

In cross-examination an interest in the case may be indicated in such a way as to weaken the evidence of the witness under cross-examination. A medical or paramedical expert witness will do no good to the case of the person on whose behalf he gives evidence if the report is 'slanted' or overtly biased in a direction favourable to that person; and such a flaw may well become apparent at this stage of the trial process.

Cross-examination by opposing counsel (that is, the barrister representing the other side) is normally polite and courteous. But the judge may always request counsel to 'rephrase the question' if he considers that the opposing counsel has been over-hostile to the expert witness.

Re-examination may then take place and any doubts which have been placed on the witness's evidence in cross-examination may be removed or resolved. If, in the case of an expert witness, any inexperience, unfamiliarity or bias has been alleged during cross-examination, re-examination is the stage at which to re-establish the credibility and stature of the witness. No leading questions may be put during re-examination, nor may questions be put at this stage which ought to have been put during the examination in chief.

ORAL EXPLANATION OF DOCUMENTARY EVIDENCE

When expert evidence is exchanged between the parties to the action before trial it may be that agreement can be reached at that stage as to the issue of liability, or as to the amount of damages, or as to both these matters. If agreement can be reached as to both then the action can be settled without recourse to litigation. Most claims for damages in respect of personal injuries are settled in this way. Approval by the court of a settlement is not required except in the case of a person under a legal disability, namely a minor or a mental patient.

There are, however, cases in which, though the contents of expert medical reports are agreed between the parties to an action, liability or damages are still contested. The interest of paramedical practitioners in such cases is in the strong comments of a judge in one case where evidence was alleged to have been agreed but was in fact far from clear in meaning. It should again be recalled that an expert's function in providing evidence on scientific or technical matters is not to state a conclusion to the case but to assist the court in reaching one. Though judges become experienced in technical matters, the case may always arise in which the presence of an expert witness who can give a helpful oral explanation of 'agreed' documentary evidence is desired by the judge.

In *Jones v. Griffith* (1969) the claim involved grand mal epilepsy, partial deafness and ear pain following a motor accident. The Court of Appeal found itself involved in guesswork as to what amount of damages to award to the injured plaintiff, and the judges had only the documentary evidence of medical experts to go by – even though the parties to the action had themselves agreed on the contents of this evidence. Commenting on the absence of oral expert evidence to explain the contents and implications of the medical evidence, Lord Justice Harman said:[2]

> I deplore the absence from the witness box of the medical advisers, who sent in their reports, it is true, but were not presented to the court so that they could be asked questions on them, which are so often so illuminating to the judge. Reports

> couched in terms of jargon are I think of no use to the court at all: they are merely the raw material on which the medical evidence should be based; and when that raw material is of a highly technical and very difficult nature it seems to me quite wrong that the chief witness on the neurological side should not have been put into the box in order that he might help the judge out of this morass of difficulties.

Clarity of explanation is expected of an expert witness in the efficient and just resolution of a liability claim involving personal injuries. If possible, the clarity and self-sufficiency of the evidence should lie in the presentation of documentary evidence (expert reports) supplied by the practitioner. But presence in court to supplement written evidence by oral explanation may be essential if justice is to be done.

MEDICAL EVIDENCE IN APPEALED CASES

It may sometimes happen that one party to an action for personal injuries appeals against an award, or refusal of an award, of damages. The interesting question then arises as to the attitude of appeal court judges to evidence which the trial judge has heard when the case was first decided, and which they have not heard from the experts themselves.

In the case of *Joyce v. Yeomans* (1981) the Court of Appeal decided that although the demeanour of medical expert witnesses is not as important, in assessing the balance of evidence, as that of other witnesses of fact, it was nevertheless material for the purpose of assessing the value of their evidence. That is to say, the way in which the oral evidence of medical witnesses is presented to a trial judge hearing the whole case, and the clarity and conviction with which that evidence is given, are important matters.

The Court of Appeal was hearing an appeal from a judge's award of damages to a 10-year-old boy who had received head injuries in a road accident. Two doctors giving evidence on his behalf stated that in their opinion the epilepsy of which the boy subsequently complained was the result of the accident. But a doctor called by the defence stated that in his opinion the boy had been a potential epileptic from birth and that the accident had merely accelerated the onset of his fits, which would in any event probably have started by the time he was 14. The judge accepted this defence evidence and assessed damages accordingly, obviously at a lower figure than that which would have been awarded were the plaintiff's expert evidence to have been accepted.

The plaintiff's lawyers contended in their appeal from this decision that the judge's finding as to the cause of the epilepsy should be reversed because it was against the weight of the evidence. They further argued that a trial judge does not have any significant advantage over the Court of Appeal in forming a correct judgement between conflicting views. The appeal judges disagreed, however, and found no reason to fault the finding of the trial judge. An appeal court, they said, ought not lightly to interfere with the findings of a trial judge on such evidence since he had the advantage of seeing and hearing the witnesses.

That is not to say that an appeal court will never interfere with a trial judge's decision on the basis of medical evidence. In *Stojalowski v. Imperial Smelting Corp.* (1976), in a claim for damages for personal injuries, the defendants contended that symptoms of severe dementia amounted to malingering. The judge had been faced with conflicting medical evidence, but had accepted the written evidence of a senior registrar and had concluded that the plaintiff was indeed malingering. His decision was overturned on appeal, and the appeal judges decided that the trial judge had given excessive weight to the written evidence. His conclusion, they held, was in the circumstances mistaken and he should have accepted the evidence of other medical witnesses in favour of the plaintiff.

Lord Justice Waller said that an allegation of malingering is a charge of fraud and requires positive evidence from the defendants of such an allegation to be put to any witness affected. It can be seen that, while malingering is something which if substantiated counts strongly against the plaintiff in whom it is alleged, the question for the trial judge is to consider whether, on the balance of evidence, such an allegation is itself supported in the first place. And since it is a charge of fraud, the evidence will have to weigh very heavily indeed against a plaintiff in whom it is alleged.

PRE-TRIAL DISCLOSURE OF EVIDENCE

It will be recalled that the giving of expert evidence constitutes an exception to the general rule that witnesses are called to testify as to the facts in issue in the case and not as to their opinion. Therefore, except when the court gives specific permission or when the parties to the action agree, expert evidence may be adduced at the trial only when an order from the court for directions as to the use of such evidence has been applied for and obtained. Such an order specifies how and under what conditions the expert evidence may be used.

Practitioners, and especially those in the remedial professions, are likely to be principally interested in cases involving claims for damages in respect of personal injuries. This section and that which follows focus attention on expert medical (including paramedical) evidence. In personal injury cases a number of special rules apply to pre-trial disclosure of the substance of medical expert evidence and the number of permitted witnesses. These rules are discussed in this section. Claims in respect of personal injuries alleged to have resulted from negligent medical (including paramedical) treatment attract the application of further special rules about disclosure of evidence and witnesses. Such cases are reserved for separate discussion in the following section of this chapter.

The party wishing to adduce expert evidence must comply with the terms of the order for directions. Orders may, and in some cases will, provide for mutual disclosure of the substance of oral and (if it is not intended to call the writer of a report as a witness) documentary medical evidence at the trial. A limit may, and in some cases will, be placed on the number of expert witnesses who will be allowed to be called to give oral evidence.

It was formerly the case that an expert medical opinion or report prepared specifically for the purpose of pending or contemplated civil proceedings and given to the legal adviser of one of the parties for that purpose was privileged against disclosure. That is, it would not be ordered to be produced to the other side before the trial or hearing, nor during the proceedings themselves.

This common law privilege is, be it noted, distinct from the legal professional privilege in evidential matters which attaches directly to the lawyer-client relationship. Legal professional privilege is discussed below.

The common law privilege preventing a court from ordering a pre-trial exchange of medical reports was substantially nullified by the introduction in 1974 of Rules of the Supreme Court giving courts[3] the power to order the parties to an action to exchange accounts of the substance of any oral or (if the maker of a report is not intended to be called) documentary expert medical evidence as a precondition to allowing the expert evidence to be given in court.

The privilege still exists, however, in a vestigial form and is still important in relation to the ability to withhold expert evidence unfavourable to the party obtaining it and therefore not intended to be used. Such evidence will not be ordered to be disclosed and will therefore remain unknown to the other party to the action unless it is later voluntarily disclosed by the party who obtained it. Nor need expert medical evidence upon which reliance is intended to be placed at the trial be disclosed if, under the Rules of the Supreme Court to be discussed below, the court, where it has a discretion in the matter, exercises its discretion against disclosure.

MEDICAL EVIDENCE IN PERSONAL INJURY CASES

Special rules relating to pre-trial disclosure of expert medical evidence apply in these cases. So common was it in personal injury actions for certain forms of direction to be given that, in order to save time spent in applying for an order for directions which would in most cases be common, the Rules of the Supreme Court introduced a new form of direction in 1980. Unless there is an application for a different form of direction as to disclosure and witnesses (mentioned below), the following direction shall take effect automatically.

There shall be mutual disclosure of documents relating to the case; where any party intends to place reliance at the trial on expert evidence he shall disclose the substance of that evidence to the other parties in the form of a written report; and this report shall if possible be agreed.

If expert reports are not so agreed, the parties shall be at liberty to call as expert witnesses those witnesses the substance of whose evidence has been disclosed before the trial. The number of expert witnesses to be called at the trial to give oral evidence shall be limited in any case to two medical experts and one expert of any other kind. For the purpose of 'medical' testimony, paramedical practitioners will be counted as medical expert witnesses if their expert evidence takes the form of specialist professional expertise. 'Medical' evidence depends rather upon the nature of the evidence than upon the specific profession of the expert witness called upon to give it. Paramedical practitioners may thus be included within the term 'medical experts' for this purpose.

This rule as to automatic disclosure and the specified limit upon the number of witnesses permitted to give oral evidence does not apply to any action in which the pleadings contain an allegation of a negligent act or omission in the course of medical treatment.

Because this procedure is automatic it is unnecessary to make an application for an order for directions to be given. It may be, however, that one of the parties does not wish for the effects of this automatic procedure. Perhaps, for instance, the limitation on the number of witnesses is not desired. In that case a separate application can be made in respect of oral expert evidence to be adduced at the trial. Under this procedure the court shall direct that the substance of the evidence sought to be adduced at the trial be disclosed in writing on such terms as the court may specify.

An exception exists if the court considers there is a 'sufficient reason' for not doing so. Where the expert evidence relates to medical matters, the court may in its discretion decline to order disclosure if such evidence contains an opinion as to the way in which personal injuries were sustained, or an opinion as to whether the injured plaintiff is malingering. This rule as to disclosure, requiring disclosure save in these two exceptional cases, does not apply to allegations of medical negligence or malpractice.

ALLEGATIONS OF MEDICAL NEGLIGENCE

Neither of the above procedures, the one automatically ordering pre-trial disclosure of the substance of medical evidence and the other requiring the court so to order unless a sufficient reason exists for not doing so, applies in a case where the pleadings reveal an allegation of negligence in medical treatment. The case of *Rahman v. Kirklees Area Health Authority* (1980) is instructive on the attitude of a court to pre-trial disclosure in a medical negligence case.

The case involved an allegation that the plaintiff was subjected to delivery of her child by caesarean section which, if it could not have been avoided altogether by the exercise of proper diagnostic skill, was at any rate not carried out at the right time or at all, before the death of the baby. The events were alleged to have occurred owing to a want of proper supervision of the patient. In connection with the plaintiff's summons for directions a judge ordered that there should be no pre-trial disclosure of the substance of experts' oral evidence. The judge also ordered that there should be no limitation on the number of medical witnesses to be called on either side. The plaintiff appealed to the Court of Appeal against both these orders, but her appeal was dismissed on both counts and the judge's order upheld.

In respect of disclosure, or rather the absence of it, Lord Justice Ormrod said:[4]

> Expert evidence in an action for medical negligence or for professional negligence takes on an entirely different character, because the evidence is directed not to what the patient's condition is now or was as a result of the accident or what it is going to be in the course of time in order that damages can be assessed. The expert evidence in this case is directed to the crucial question: was the treatment correct or reasonable in the circumstances. That is an enormous difference.

The reason for putting medical negligence cases in a class apart for the purposes of considering disclosure is that it is common for the defendant's expert in a medical negligence case to be given proofs of the evidence of those whose acts and omissions are under scrutiny so as to form his expert opinion. Disclosure of the defendant's expert's report would therefore in effect disclose to the other side a summary of the defendant's proofs of evidence. In other words it could give the whole show away before the actual trial.

As regards the number of witnesses, and the refusal of the court in this case to place a limit on their number, Lord Justice Cumming-Bruce said:[5]

> The judge decided not to limit the number of witnesses. Counsel for the plaintiff submits that that is onerous and subjects the plaintiff, a mere patient, to the prospect of litigation in which a whole string of men of medical learning may be marshalled to follow each other into the witness box to obscure the truth out of a misguided sense of loyalty to a member or members of their profession charged with negligence. The history of medical negligence actions, I think, can be said to show that counsel's apprehensions are not wholly fanciful but, as against that, this court should not approach a case on the basis that the defendants, a public authority, will consciously try to abuse their position.

To this Lord Justice Ormrod added:[6]

> In a case like this I do not, for my part, see any useful purpose whatever in limiting the number of witnesses. If the defendants or plaintiff try to abuse the position by calling an innumerable number of witnesses they may well end up by damaging their own case in nine out of ten cases, and the trial judge can deal with it himself.

THE EXPERT'S FUNCTION IN MEDICAL NEGLIGENCE CASES

One further comment is required on the role of the medical expert in cases involving an allegation of negligence against a medical or paramedical practitioner, in addition to the practice affecting pre-trial orders as to disclosure of witnesses.

As was indicated earlier in this chapter in more general terms, an expert's medical opinion in a case involving an allegation of medical negligence should avoid being clearly partisan or 'slanted'. In the case of *Whitehouse v. Jordan* (1981), which involved an allegation of medical negligence, the following warning was issued by Lord Wilberforce:[7]

> I have to say that I feel some concern as to the manner in which part of the expert evidence called for the plaintiff came to be organised . . . While some degree of consultation between experts and legal advisers is entirely proper, it is necessary that expert evidence presented to the court should be, and should be seen to be, the independent product of the expert, uninfluenced as to form or content by the exigencies of litigation.

LEGAL PROFESSIONAL PRIVILEGE

While the subject of legal professional privilege against disclosure is one involving considerable case law and rules, it is not necessary to discuss it here at any great length, for one simple reason. That is, that while communications passing between lawyer and client are immune from disclosure in legal proceedings, communications between medical or paramedical practitioner and patient or client are not. Thus medical and paramedical practitioners are compellable witnesses who may be ordered by subpoena or witness summons to attend court and give evidence, and to produce documents such as case notes which are in their possession, custody or control. Medical and paramedical practitioners in the witness box cannot refuse to answer a question on grounds of professional privilege – there is no such privilege.

Nevertheless there are strong indications that the courts will not treat the absence of privilege against disclosing or revealing communications as a reason for always insisting on the medical or paramedical practitioner's disclosure. In the case of *Attorney-General v. Mulholland* (1963) Lord Denning shed some light on the likely practice of the courts. The case did not in fact involve such practitioners and his words are not part of a binding precedent. Nevertheless their meaning and import are clear:[8]

> The only profession that I know which is given a privilege from disclosing information to a court of law is the legal profession, and then it is not the privilege of the lawyer but of his client. Take the clergyman, the banker or the medical man. None of these is entitled to refuse to answer when directed to by a judge. Let me not be mistaken. The judge will respect the confidences which each member of these honourable professions receives in the course of it, and will not direct him to answer unless not only it is relevant but also it is a proper and, indeed, necessary question in the course of justice to be put and answered.

A final word should be added under this heading about the status of experts' reports, prepared for the purpose of pending or contemplated civil proceedings. It was noted earlier in this chapter that the privilege which used to exist in respect of medical reports given to the legal advisers of a party to pending or contemplated proceedings was considerably curtailed in its effect following the introduction, in 1974, of Rules of the Supreme Court permitting and in some cases directing the pre-trial disclosure of medical reports or the substance of oral expert evidence to be given in court. Such a case involves a three-party relationship. However, even in the two-party solicitor-client relationship in which legal professional privilege typically exists, limits are placed on the availability of the privilege.

The case of *Waugh v. British Railways Board* (1979) involved a fatal accident to a railway worker. In accordance with the Board's usual practice an internal inquiry report was prepared and headed 'For the information of the Board's solicitor'. One of the purposes of the report was to establish the cause of the accident in order to take appropriate safety measures. The plaintiff, the widow of the deceased railway worker, desired disclosure of the report as it was probably the best available evidence as to the cause of the accident.

On appeal to the House of Lords from a refusal to direct disclosure on grounds of legal professional privilege, the Law Lords decided that a document is to be accorded privilege from production on the ground of legal professional privilege only if the sole or dominant purpose for which it is prepared is that of submitting it to a legal advisor for advice and use in litigation. It therefore followed that the accident report in that case was not privileged against the desired disclosure.

Paramedical practitioners could conceivably become involved in such an issue in two ways. Those working in a hospital or similar institution might be required to testify as to the cause of an accident on the premises. Or they might themselves, in an unfortunate instance, be victims of an accident in respect of which an internal inquiry is held. In the latter case the chances of success of such a practitioner-victim in applying for disclosure of an inquiry report would be similar to those of the plaintiff in the above case, and based on the same grounds as to the sole or dominant purpose of the inquiry report.

DISCLOSURE OF DOCUMENTS FOR OTHER REASONS

Subject to claims of legal professional privilege as just described, there remain for discussion two further reasons for which disclosure of documents may be requested by a party and required or ordered by a court. The Supreme Court Act 1981 gives the courts certain powers to order disclosure of documents in two different situations. First, where a person appears to the High Court to be likely to be a party to subsequent proceedings in which a claim in respect of personal injuries or death is likely to be made, the court has power to order another person, who appears to be likely to be a party to the proceedings and to have or have had in his possession, custody or control, any documents relevant to an issue arising or likely to arise out of that claim, to disclose whether he has those documents and to produce those as are in his possession, custody or control (section 33).

The expression 'likely to be made' in respect of a death or personal injuries claim was widely interpreted in the case of *Dunning v. Board of Governors of the United Liverpool Hospitals* (1973). The court held that the words are to be construed as meaning 'may' or 'may well be' made if, on examination, the documents (including medical records) indicate that the applicant for disclosure has a good cause of action.

A further power, framed in very similar language, enables a court, on the application of a party to proceedings which have already begun, to order disclosure of documents such as medical records against someone who is not a party to those proceedings (section 34).

In both these different instances of an order to produce documents and records the courts are given a discretion by the Supreme Court Act 1981 to order production, but to someone other than the applicant himself. Such production may be to the applicant's legal advisers; or to his legal advisers *and* medical or other professional advisers; or, if the applicant for disclosure has no legal advisers, to any medical or other professional advisers alone.

PRESERVATION OF PUBLIC RECORDS

Hospital and health authority records fall within the meaning of 'public records' for the purposes of the Public Records Act 1958 and are records for which the DHSS is responsible.

Health circular HN(61)73 instructs health authorities as to which records should be permanently retained and as to which might be destroyed and after how long. The Act places a positive duty on health authorities to segregate and take proper care of documents which ought to be permanently preserved. The Act prohibits the destruction of any documents dated earlier than 1660, and the 1961 circular gives guidance on which documents of more recent date should be preserved and states that any document created before 1858 should always be preserved.

REFERENCES

[1] For an excellent account of the practical aspects of medical testimony see: Pearce, G. H. (1979). *The Medical Report and Testimony*. George Allen and Unwin, London.
[2] [1969] 2 All E.R. 1015, p. 1020
[3] Such powers are given to the County Courts in like cases also.
[4] [1980] 3 All E.R. 610, p. 614
[5] op. cit., p. 613
[6] op. cit., pp. 614–16
[7] [1981] 1 All E.R. 267, p. 276
[8] [1963] 1 All E.R. 767, p. 771

TABLE OF STATUTES

TABLE OF STATUTORY INSTRUMENTS

TABLE OF CASES

SELECT BIBLIOGRAPHY

The Hospitals and Health Services Year Book. Institute of Health Service Administrators, 75 Portland Place, London W1N 4AN. (Published annually)

Bluglass, R. (1983). *A Guide to the Mental Health Act 1983*. Churchill Livingstone, Edinburgh.

Finch, J. D. (1981). *Health Services Law*. Sweet and Maxwell, London.

Gostin, L. (1983). *A Practical Guide to Mental Health Law. The Mental Health Act 1983 and Related Legislation*. MIND, London.

Guthrie, D. (ed) (1981). *Disability Legislation and Practice*. Macmillan Press, London.

Mason, J. K. and McCall-Smith, A. (1983). *Law and Medical Ethics*. Butterworths, London.

Ministry of Health (1972). *Code of Practice for the Protection of Persons Exposed to Ionizing Radiations Arising from Medical and Dental Use*. HMSO, London.

Pearce, G. H. (1979). *The Medical Report and Testimony*. George Allen and Unwin, London.

Ritson, J. (1983). *Health and Safety at Work Act*. Ravenswood Publications Limited, Beckenham, Kent.

Hickok, R. (1982). *Physical Therapy: Administration and Management*, 2nd edition, Williams and Wilkins, Baltimore.

USEFUL PROFESSIONAL ADDRESSES

Association of Dental Surgery Assistants
DSA House, 29 London Street
Fleetwood, Lancashire FY7 6JY

British Association of Occupational Therapists
20 Rede Place, London W2 4TU 01-229 9738

British Dietetic Association
Daimler House, Paradise Street
Birmingham B1 2BJ 021-643 5483

British Orthoptic Society
Norvic House, Hilton Street
Manchester M4 1LP

Chartered Society of Physiotherapy
14 Bedford Row, London WC1R 4ED 01-242 1941

Council for Professions Supplementary to Medicine
Park House, 184 Kennington Park Road
London SE11 4BU 01-582 0866

Department of Health and Social Security
Alexander Fleming House,
London SE1 6BY 01-407 5522

European Economic Community Commission
UK Office, 20 Kensington Palace Gardens
London W8 4QQ 01-727 8090

Free Church Federal Council Hospital Chaplaincy Board
27 Tavistock Square, London WC1H 9HH 01-387 8413

Health and Safety Executive
25 Chapel Street, London NW1 5DT 01-262 3277

Health Services Management Centre
Park House, 40 Edgbaston Park Road
Birmingham B15 2RT 021-455 7511

Hospital Chaplaincies Council (Church of England)
c/o Church House, Dean's Yard
London SW1P 3NZ 01-222 9011

Institute of Medical Laboratory Sciences
12 Queen Anne Street, London W1M 0AU 01-636 8192

King's Fund Centre
126 Albert Street, London NW1 7NF 01-267 6111

The Law Society
113 Chancery Lane, London WC2 01-242 1222

NHS Training and Studies Centre
The White Hart, Cold Bath Road
Harrogate HG2 7JN 0423 55681

Pharmaceutical Society of Great Britain
1 Lambeth High Street, London SE1 7JN 01-735 9141

Society of Chiropodists
8 Wimpole Street, London W1M 8BX 01-580 3227

Society of Radiographers
14 Upper Wimpole Street, London W1M 8BN 01-935 5726

Society of Remedial Gymnasts
c/o Remedial Gymnasium, Kingston General Hospital
Hull HU3 1UR 0482 28631

Union of Speech Therapists/ASTMS
c/o 79 Camden Road, London NW1 9ES 01-267 4722

INDEX